SUNDANCING

THE ART AND ARCHITECTURE OF JAMES LAMBETH

*Warm Wishes,
James Lambeth*

Introduction by Sarah P. Harkness, FAIA

Edited by Hun Bae Im and Courtney Lambeth

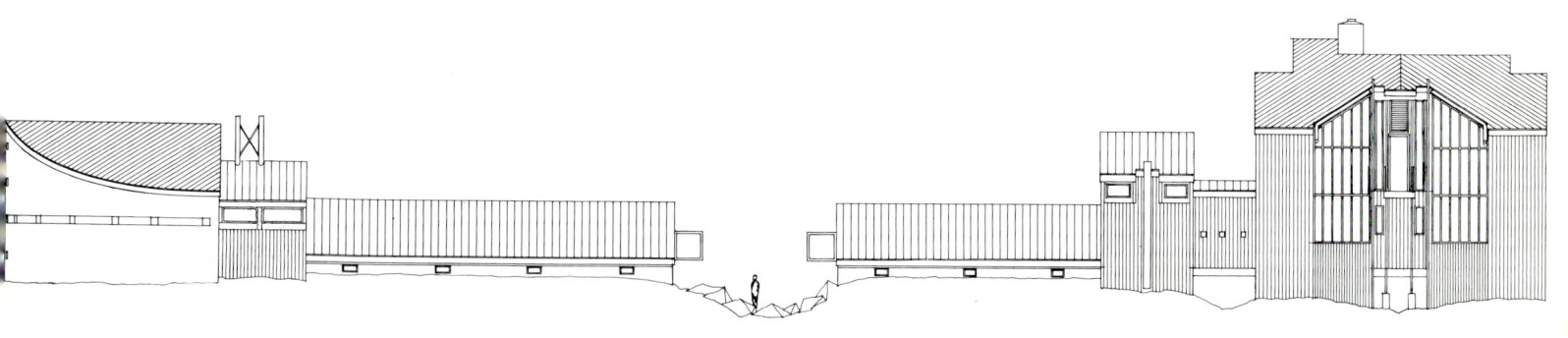

MIAMI
DOG
PRESS

Johnson, AR, USA

Copyright © 1993 Miami Dog Press. All rights reserved.
Printed in Hong Kong by Everbest Printing Co., Ltd.
through Four Colour Imports, Ltd., Louisville, KY.

First published in the United States of America in 1993 by
MIAMI • DOG • PRESS. 3906 Greathouse Springs Road,
P.O. Box 409, Johnson, AR, 72741, USA, (501) 521-1304
FAX (501) 521-8091, Order Number 1-800-538-8265

LIBRARY OF CONGRESS CATALOGING-IN-PUBLICATION DATA
Lambeth, James, 1942-
Sundancing : the art and architecture of James Lambeth/
introduction by Sarah P. Harkness : edited by Hun Bae Im
and Courtney Lambeth
p.   cm.
Includes bibliographical references.
ISBN 0-9601678-8-9 : $48. — ISBN 0-9601678-9-7 (pbk.) $38.
1. Lambeth, James, 1942- — Themes, motives. 2. Architecture, Modern — 20th century — United States — Themes,
motives. I. Harkness, Sarah P., 1929- . II. Im, Hun Bae, 1948- .
III. Lambeth, Courtney, 1968- . IV. Title.
NA737.L26A4 1992   92-60943
720'.92—dc20   CIP

Designed by James Lambeth
Type in Helios by Stafford and Associates
Edited and compiled by Courtney Lambeth and Im Hun Bae

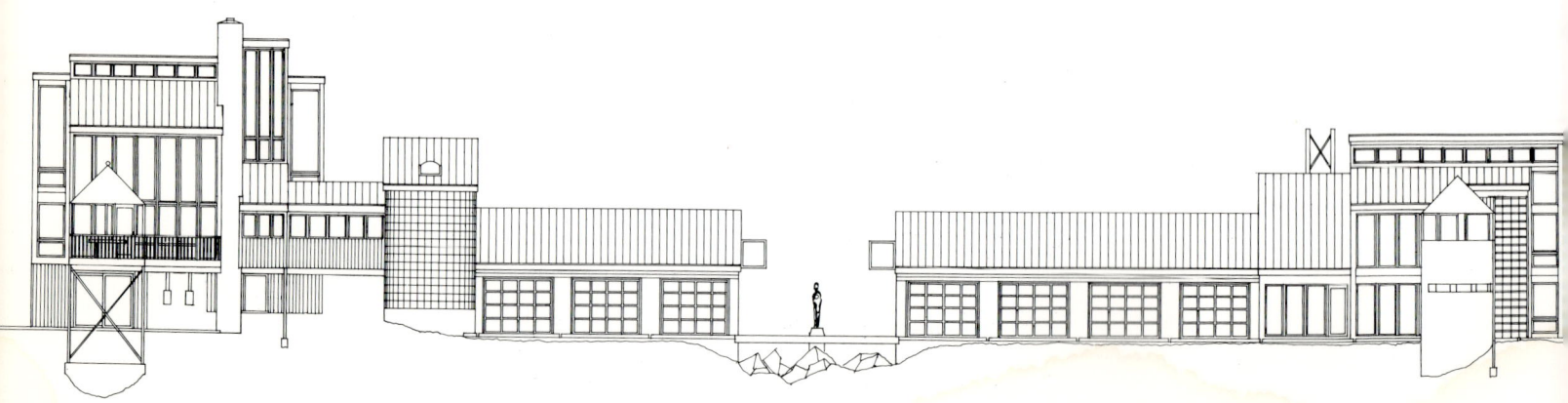

Table of Contents

Foreward by Jorg W. Ludwig	5
Preface by James Lambeth	6
Introduction by Sarah P. Harkness, FAIA	8
Mass Housing Project	14
Student Chair	15
Megastructure	16
Mass Transit Object	17
Lambeth Residence	18
Belzung Residence	26
Lushbaugh Lake House	28
Combs Residence	30
Yocum Ski Lodge	32
Solar Lens Fantasy	42
McKamey Residence	46
Misawa	50
Silver Necklace	53
Solar Module Cabin	54
Strawberry Fields East	62
Delap Residence	66
Solar Village	72
Hall Residence	76
Mobile Home	80
Spock Residence	82
Strawberry Fields West	84
Solar Pak Fantasy	85
Walker Residence	86
Hot Springs Residence	88
Dixon Residence	89
American Academy in Rome	90
Ma and Ra	91
Ospedale Dei Bambini	94
Gold Necklace	95
Sundance Paintings	96
Brady Residence	100
Sexton Towers	104
Berlin Housing	106
Eagleridge	108
Tribune Tower Update	111
Blevins High School	112
Peak	116
Sculpture Gallery	123
Desert Compound	124
Gary Lambeth Residence	130
Best Inn	132
Sphinx	134
Hedges Residence	136
Piney Grove	150
Miller Residence	152
Davenport Residence	156
Leslie Residence	158
Yeager Residence	164
Inn at the Mill	174
Lambeth Residence	188
Bibliography	204
Sun Charts	206
Acknowledgments	207
Photo Credits	207
Biography	208

To Joyce:

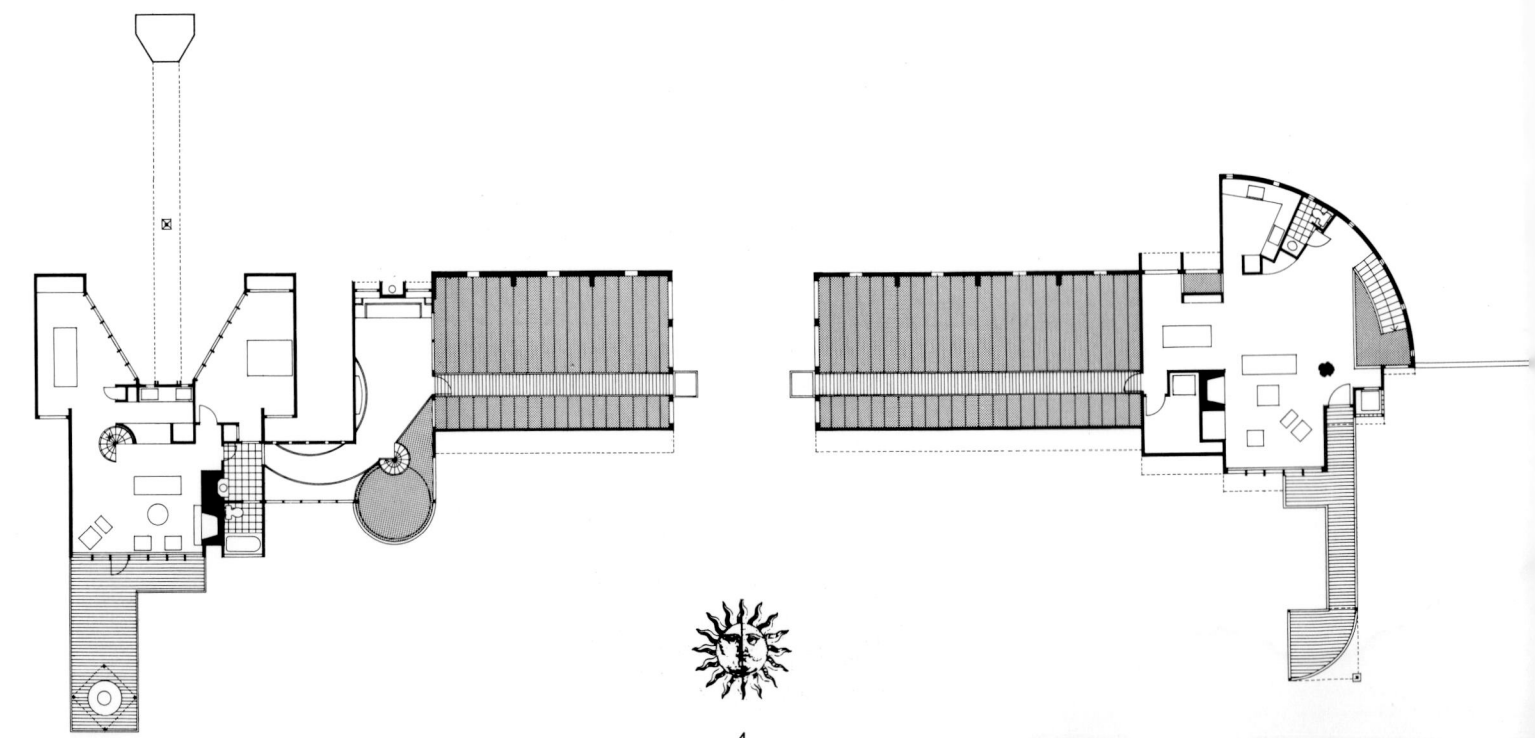

Foreward

"Amerika, Du hast es besser (America, you have it better)", this anguished and reverent cry by Johann Wolfgang Goethe, 18th-century-Germany's greatest man of letters, was frequently, if quietly uttered by many a visitor to SOLAR 4 — the exhibition of energy-conscious, climate-adaptive architectural design which James Lambeth conceived and organized for the American Cultural Center in Berlin. His work has fascinated and inspired students of architecture — young and old, urban planners and environmental activists, engineers and artists throughout Europe for over half a decade. From Rome to Kopenhagen, from London to Zagreb, this presentation of America's best solar design, proved to millions of Europeans who came to see the exhibition at American cultural centers, universities, national ministries and municipal galleries, or shared in its message through television, newspapers or professional journals, that "solar architecture" is not only responsive to our ecological, microclimatic and energy needs but can also be sensitive to our socio-cultural and aesthetic concerns.

At a time when many young Europeans associated the global problems of energy depletion, environmental degredation and run-away technology with the United States, James Lambeth, the youthful professor of architecture from America's heartland, through his work as an architect, his inspiration as a teacher, and his vision as an artist, served his country and his profession well as a most credible "Ambassador" for American ecological resolve and creative excellence.

James Lambeth's art and architecture, quintessentially American by its can-do optimism and its make-do pragmatism, is equally informed by his love for and faith in his native land and its not so short history, and by his intimate knowledge and mastery of architecture and latest technologies. He is an American Renaissance man comfortably at home in the global village.

Jorg W. Ludwig
Deputy Director
Amerika Haus, Berlin
September, 1992

Christmas Card

Preface

We shall arrive at Heathrow in less than an hour. The view through the baseball size window is breathtaking; a violet glow embracing the curve of the earth. At twice the speed of sound it's utterly quiet...beautifully peaceful. I was allowed into the cockpit a few minutes ago. The British pilots were relaxed and talkative. They took great pride in explaining the technics of the Concord's flight. They explained the concerns of their job; to go as fast as possible without melting the nose of the craft. The plane was in perfect balance; a balance that resulted in timeless beauty that transcends fad and fashion.

Sailing ships and race cars also possess this timeless esthetic. Bones and shells are shaped by the internal and external forces of nature; correct and sensual.

Architecture, too, should be a balance of the forces acting upon it. For me, the prime form giving element has always been the sun. Its predictable cycle bathes all buildings in light and energy. I felt that if a form could be shaped by this earth/sun relationship, it too would have a timeless quality.

Although the early projects were oriented to the sun, they also were shaped by a youthful desire for illusion and fantasy. Kaleospic reflective walls dazzled the entrant; requiring a kind of visual involvement with the building environment. In later designs these reflective surfaces took on a dual function of directing sun energy to specific areas at specific seasons of the year. The molding of the Art and Science of Architecture has always been my interest.

I had been working on a "solar esthetic" for a number of years before the oil embargo of the early seventies stunned America. My youthful designs had been published throughout the United States, Europe, and Asia. Overnight I was dubbed an "energy expert" and one of the new breed of American architects.

My work took on a new seriousness. There was precious little data so I set out to develop my own. I began by designing a series of one room cabins that had no external energy source other than a wood burning stove. The "solar module cabins" were built throughout the Ozark Mountains by the private sector; bankers wanting a weekend hide-a-way, journalists wanting to experience the "Solar Age," and convicts wanting a "hide out" in the remote forests of North Central Arkansas. Each project gave data for the refinement of the next. The research was unique and proved to be extremely useful.

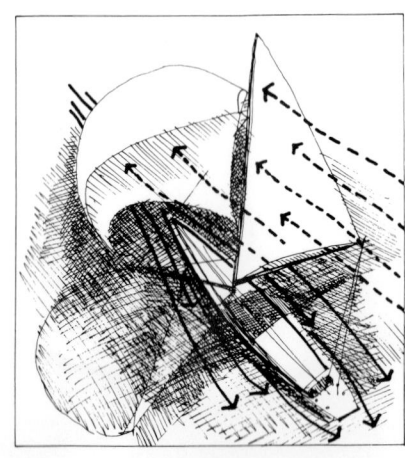

While the U.S. industries set out developing "solar hardware," funded by large government grants, a few of us continued to develop what would later be called "Passive Solar" design. There would be little funding for this "fanatic fringe" movement of energy efficient architecture. The process was not recognized by the scientific community (it was not hardware), nor was it accepted by the majority of the sluggish and somewhat defensive architectural establishment. It was not architecture, it was not engineering!

The Delap residence was the accumulation of my solar module development. A young couple needing a modest middle American home became the ideal test for the research. The resulting residence was determined by The National Science Foundation to be the most energy efficient structure built in the United States.

The first decade of work was the basis for a well received book titled "SOLAR DESIGNING." What followed was a hectic schedule of traveling and lecturing throughout the United States and Europe. I was commissioned to design an exhibition on solar architecture for Berlin's "Amerika Haus." The show toured Europe and was the most successful exhibition of the year. I then had the good fortune of winning the Prix de Roma. While in Rome I began to sketch illustrations for a children's book, "Ma and Ra." The story covered the realities and fantasies of a solar odyssey. Still fascinated by the generation of solar forms, the "Sundance" paintings were completed; classical solar sections extruded across an imaginary landscape. The decade ended and the Reagan Years began.

The fine tuned, highly efficient forms of the previous decade slowly gave way to larger and more opulant designs of the eighties. Not only was I to design the structure but also furniture, paintings, fabrics, and even jewelry for the clients.

Our sun shaped cities of the future will tell us in what direction we are traveling as well as the time of day. Buildings will be great solar sun dials with each face expressing its orientation. They will be efficient, timeless, and stunningly beautiful.

My journey is nearing the end. The old truths that I based my life's work on are still relevant; waiting to be discovered and rediscovered by a new generation.

I didn't create a "solar style" as I set out to do; but a "design process" that is an open ended beginning for form generation. The result is an architecture of the sun; efficient and based on timeless principles. The sun is the same and the philosophy is the same and once again the clouds part as the engines scream our arrival.

J.L.
New York/London
May, 1992

Introduction
by Sarah P. Harkness, FAIA

I am writing in the aftermath of the Earth Summit that took place in Rio de Janeiro in June, 1992.

The purpose of the Earth Summit was to promote "environmentally sound and life-sustaining development in all countries." Whether or not it is possible to couple environmentally sound technologies with economic growth of the kind we are used to — to have one's cake and eat it, too — may be a question. "Life-sustaining development" will have to be different from what we think of as "development". And our fear of Nature (wolves howling in the night) must be overcome. But finally, we will not be convinced of a new way of life unless it includes the aesthetic lift of delight.

This is where James Lambeth's architecture comes in. Lambeth's guiding light is the sun. He lives and works with the sun, plays with it, and looks to it for inspiration. Like a partner, the sun is an influence in all of his work. Lambeth does not belong to the back-to-the-earth, hair shirt school of design that finds expression in shaggy architecture of the past. Instead, new materials and technologies join in the game of design. This is modern design in its true sense — rational solutions, cleancut and functional. In this case, geometry and fantasy also play together, always instructed by the sun.

SUNDANCING covers 25 years of architectural practice. As could be expected, projects in the later years are usually larger, more developed, and in some cases a little more sober. A comparison of the Solar Module Cabins (1974) with the Leslie house (1991) is interesting.

The Solar Module Cabins could be seen as built diagrams, as basic in design to catch the sun as the Pueblo cliff dwellings in the Southwest (so much admired and analyzed by solar experts).

The Leslie house has a new look, but design is still driven by the sun. The south facing tall funnel shape of the cabins and of some of the early houses has broadened into a wide, linear scoop of rooms

Cliff Dwelling

directed south around the terrace and pool of the Leslie house. Spacially, some of the early houses seem to take off into the mountains; the Leslie house stays still. Instead of spatial drama, it revels in elegant materials (polished marble walls and floors) and sophisticated furniture design (leather and onyx settees in the entrance hall).

In every project shown in this book we see Lambeth's fascination with the geometry of sunlight, direct and reflected. The mirrored surface that heats the pool which then reflects into the interior of the Combs house, the lens that melts the snow at the front door of the Yocum Ski Lodge, and the long, curved reflector (surfaced with prismatic aluminum mylar) that doubles the efficiency of the hot water solar collector of the Blevins High School, are technical inventions. But they are also aesthetic inventions. The reflectors take on color, depending on the time of day, and all devices are part of the architecture, not add-ons. Lambeth delights in the use of shiny, rich materials, which often appear as surprises in a building whose simple exterior is so much part of the wilderness. (I'm reminded of a crow who collects objects that glint and glitter to decorate its nest).

What can we learn from this architecture? Without such glorious sites to work with, how can other architects do the same? And what about larger buildings, more than one room deep? There are many ways to bring about "environmentally sound and life-sustaining development," and as many ways to make that development aesthetically pleasing. Lambeth shows us that solar design can be dramatic, as well as pleasing. His design follows a very personal avenue in a very special part of the world; other designers will find other solutions and other expressions. It is good to know that Lambeth's senior partner, the sun, will not only live forever, but is available for consultation.

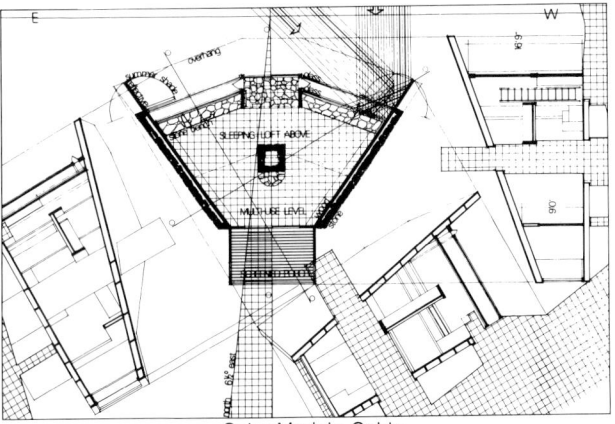
Solar Module Cabin

THE SOLAR SECTION:
STARTING POINT OF PASSIVE DESIGN
Sarah P. Harkness, AIA JOURNAL, January 1981

Solar design is not always apparent, especially when the passive approach is taken. Neither does it dictate any particular style. However, the sun makes its own terms, and they must be acknowledged. The response to these terms is most apparent in sections of solar buildings, most particularly in south-north sections. For better or for worse, this is where the designer must begin.

Throughout history people have rediscovered the south-facing cave shape. From Socrates (469-399 B.C.) in Greece to James Lambeth in present day Arkansas, designers have come up with the same semicircular or trapezoidal sun trap. When an idea comes up again and again, one wonders if it is a typical blind alley or if there is something universal about it. Why has the form not become common? In solar architecture, the cave shape is the purest example of direct gain, catching not only the direct south sun, but the east and west sun as it hits the angled walls. Perhaps one answer is simply that an angular or curved building is usually not as economical to build or as logical for planning purposes as a rectangular one.

If we assume, then, that a rectangular plan is almost as good a sun catcher as the trapezoidal plan, we see that the same section "invented" by Socrates — the shed roof opening to the south with a balcony hung in the high space of a heat absorbing or thermal mass type of structure — is a basic form in solar architecture. Closed by glass at the south opening, the form is especially prevalent in adobe construction in New Mexico. Since the climate is reliably sunny in the daytime and cool at night, in winter the thermal mass of the building, insulated on the outside or banked with earth like a cave, absorbs daytime heat, thereby preventing it from overheating, and gives up the heat at night when the outside air temperature goes down.

Nighttime window insulation prevents heat loss through the glass. In summer the overhanging roof cuts off the direct sun into the space. Since warm air rises, there are different "climates" at dif-

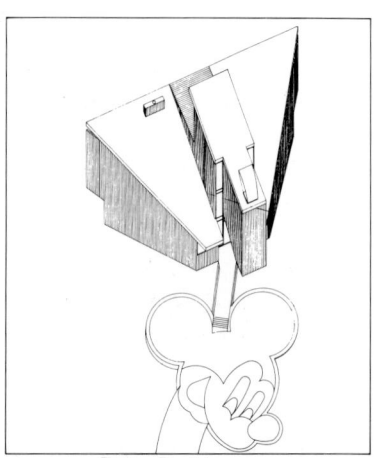

Delap Residence

ferent levels in the building at different times of day, which may dictate how many spaces are used, or may cause a migration of use from one part of the building to another in the course of a day.

Returning to the original cave shape, James Lambeth has exploited it in ways that suggest further possibilities. Lambeth's design for an isolated vacation cabin in Hazel Valley, Ark., is a pure and simple example of a passive solar dwelling. As well as glass at the south opening, sophisticated improvements to the south-facing trapezoidal form include thermal walls set back from the glass at each end of the south window wall, an open stone fireplace which also absorbs radiation from the sun and two-story hinged wall reflectors to increase the sunlight hitting the thermal storage walls. The roof and east and west walls are highly insulated between the thermal layer and the outside wall, and the concrete floor also acts as thermal mass.

The Delap residence by Lambeth, built in 1977 in Fayetteville, Ark., is designed on the same concept as the cabin, but is developed into a three-bedroom family house. Carrying the concept further, Lambeth has developed hypothetical schemes for housing, where unit modules, designed to prove 75 percent of internal climate control without any mechanical devices, could be plugged into geometric groupings. "A combination of large amounts of insulated glass and limited interior volume produced the form," Lambeth explains.

Variations on the solar cave shape have been designed and built independently in different parts of the country. A typical variation is a trapezoidal greenhouse with thermal mass side and back walls, set within a rectangular or other shape of building. Heat absorbed by the back and side walls is given off at night to the surrounding living spaces. A notion occurs that the trapezoidal sun spaces might be nested with trapezoidal shapes facing north to develop a plan system for a larger building. Beginning with an understanding of the original solar cave, possibilities are endless.

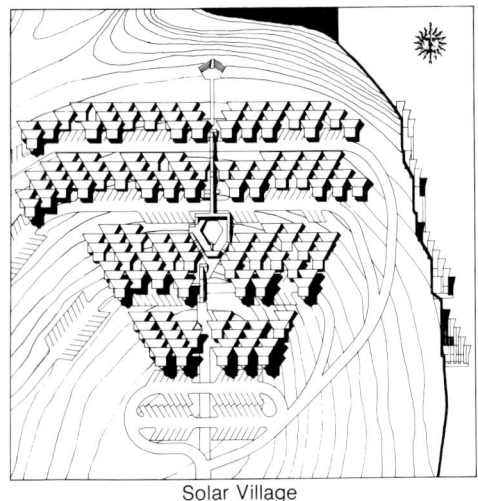

Solar Village

SUNDANCING

"The Sun Dance was a tribal event of considerable magnitude. Sometime during the summer months of each year the bands and clans assembled at an appointed place. Here a great Sun Lodge was built according to traditional rules, and the men who had made their vows fulfilled them by pulling against thongs which secured them by their chests to the Sun Pole, which stood at the center of the lodge, until at last they either pulled or were cut free. Such painful rites were always carried out on behalf of the tribe and because of this all of the people shared in the event, looking upon it as a holy and a joyful occasion. It did relatively little damage to the warriors most directly involved, and the Indians, to this day, are not able to understand why the Sun Dance Ceremony, which was so important to them, vexed the White man so that once he dominated them he forced its abandonment."

Thomas E. Mails, THE MISTIC WARRIORS OF THE PLAINS

Selected Projects
1966 - 1992

Mass Housing Project
New Delhi, India, 1966, Latitude 28.37N

Community site model

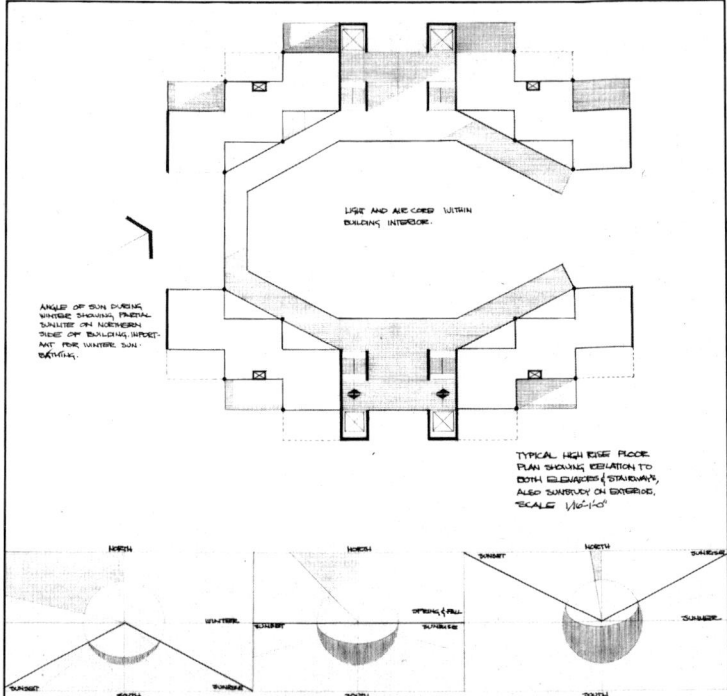
New Delhi sun charts

View into green space

This early project shows Lambeth's use of sun charts to determine architectural form. These New Delhi apartments are designed as huge cooling towers. All of the units open to an interior shaded air shaft as well as exterior balconies. The balconies are on alternating levels to keep evening radiated heat from warming lower and upper decks.

The housing complex keeps auto traffic separate from elevated pedestrian parks.

Student Chair
Washington University, Saint Louis, Missouri, 1967

This lounge chair was designed and built by Lambeth while a student at Washington University. The stainless steel frame, leather straps, and cushions disassemble and are scaled to fit the trunk of his Corvette. Architectural Critic: Hans Hollein

Top · Detail · Detail · Top

Megastructure Research Project
East Saint Louis, Illinois, 1968, Latitude 38.41N

Transit terminal perspective

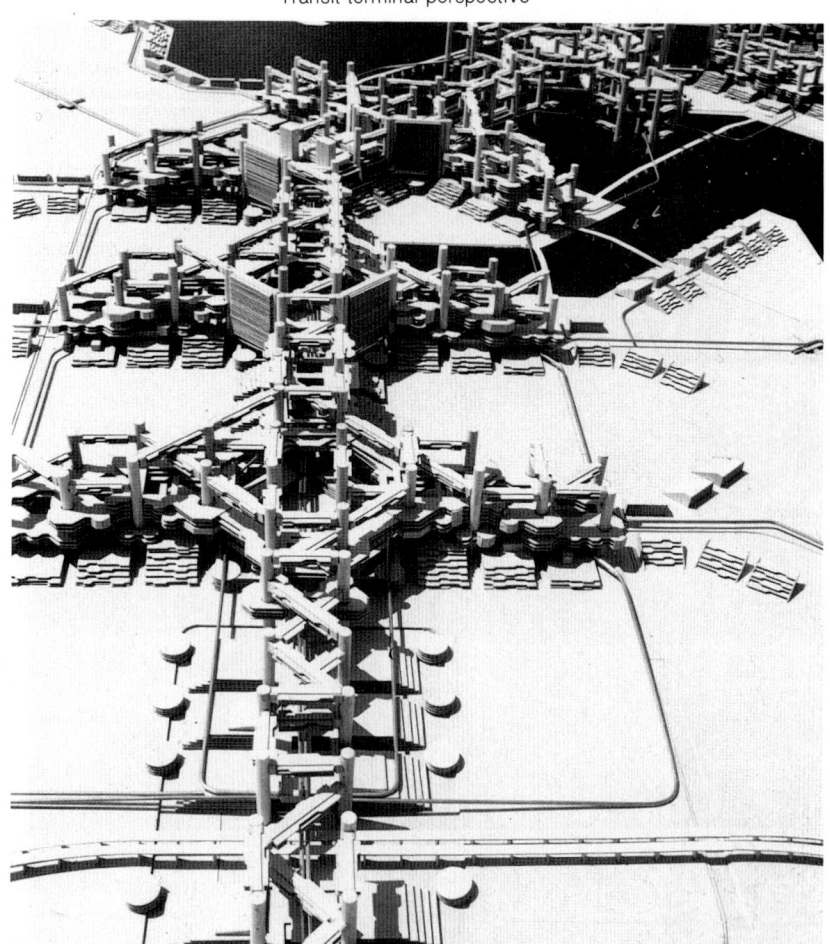

Site model

While at the University of Arkansas, Professor Lambeth and Professor Mort Karp designed this megastructure with a team of architectural students. The project was funded by the American Iron and Steel Institute. Design consultant: Moshe Safdie

Mass Transit Object
University of Arkansas, Fayetteville, Arkansas, 1968

"The photographs and drawings which follow describe an envelope of planes by James Lambeth, Professor of Architecture at the University of Arkansas, as the visual focus of an architectural conference held at the University on April 19 and 20 of this year.

Intended as an experiential objectification of the nature of the total environment that contemporary architecture must be, the effect of the envelope was so powerfully out of all proportion to the commonplace quality of the individual elements (a billboard poster, wood panels and lights) that the total effect on the observer was that of a genuine work of art.

The envelope, a wrap-around reality, is static, but the slipped and shifted planes of which it is composed imply movement. Looking at it, real people standing near the envelope, entering or leaving it, merge with the people in the photograph, requiring an observer to constantly readjust the balance of relationships between what he is seeing, and what he knows exists.

Space and movement, light and dark, combine so that when you stand still, the envelope moves; when you move, the envelope stands still. I believe that the 'Mass Transit Object' should be seen by a wider audience for it is a serious development in today's art formation."

Professor Eleanor Karp, PROGRESSIVE ARCHITECTURE

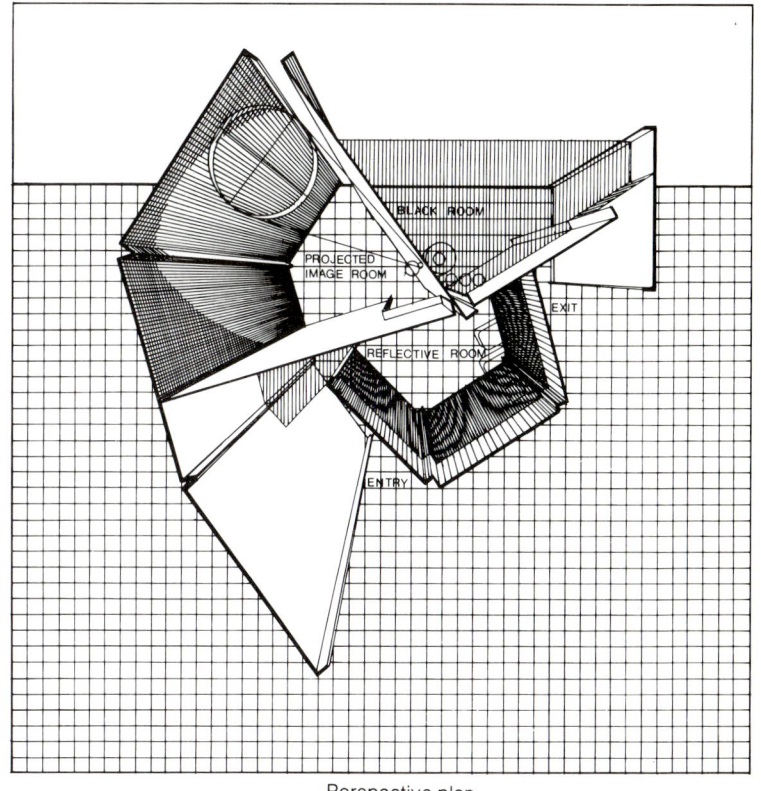

Perspective plan

View of entry

Lambeth Residence
Fayetteville, Arkansas, 1969, Latitude 36.03N

"Situated on the crest of an Ozark mountain ridge, the house is on a north south axis with entry elevation on the north side and two stories of south glass on the south side. Lambeth based the design of his own house on a "pursuit for human involvement in both real and illusionary architectural space." He leads the observer through a special entry sequence of multiple reflected images on gold mirror glass walls that flank both sides of the entry bridge.

The entry level is one level above the living area, and opens onto a two story space that affords a generous view of the Ozark mountains to the south. Children's bedroom and guest bedroom are entered off either side of the public entry. The outside wall of each bedroom on the entry level, the dining room and master bedroom below are gold mirror glass and open on to a one way view of the entry bridge and the reflected image of the opposite wall.

The outside is made part of the living area by a two story south glass wall. The glass wall has the double function of making the landscape part of the living room whie letting the warmth from the low winter sun into the living spaces.

As the family art collection played an important part of the interior design, walls are kept in a neutral tone by the use of light painted walls and hardwood floors. Lambeths wife Joyce is responsible for the tapestry."

PROCESS ARCHITECTURE #6, 1978

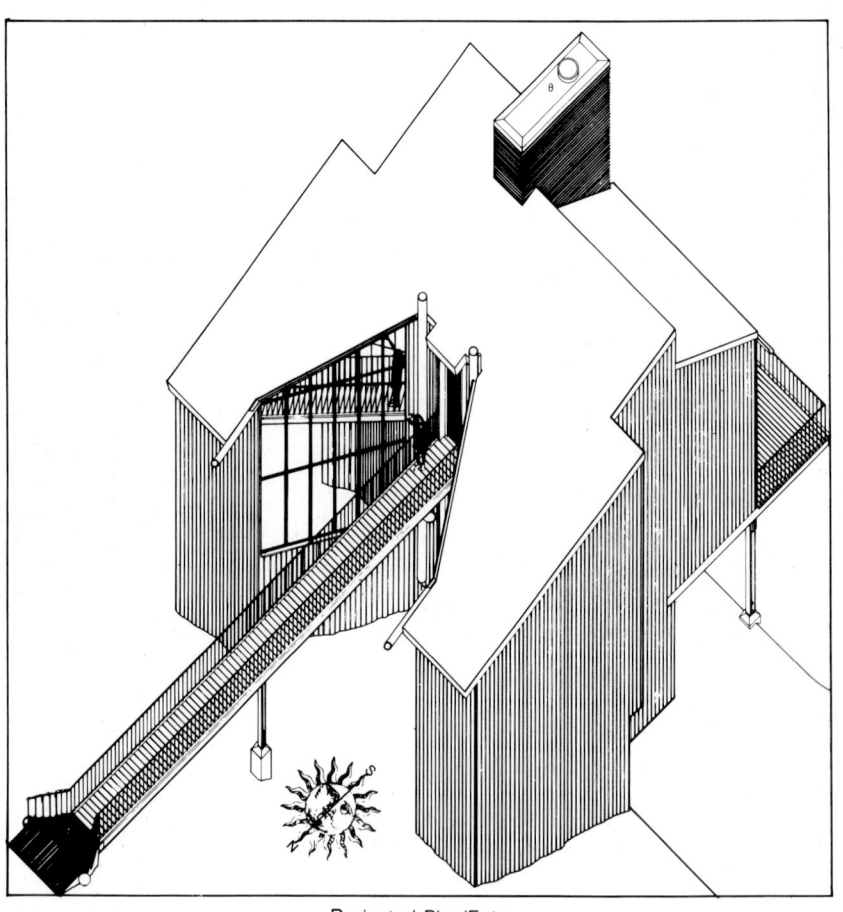

Projected Plan/Entry

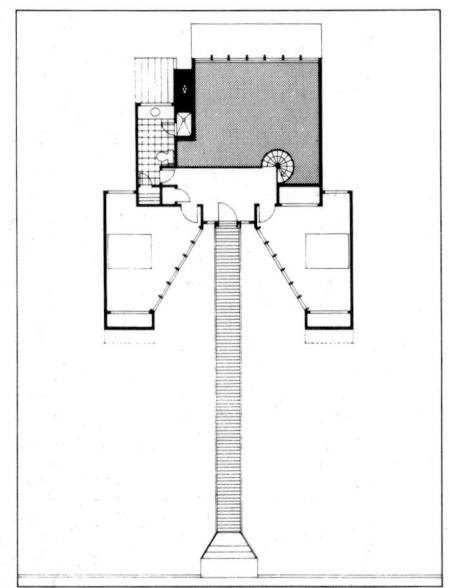

Third Floor Plan

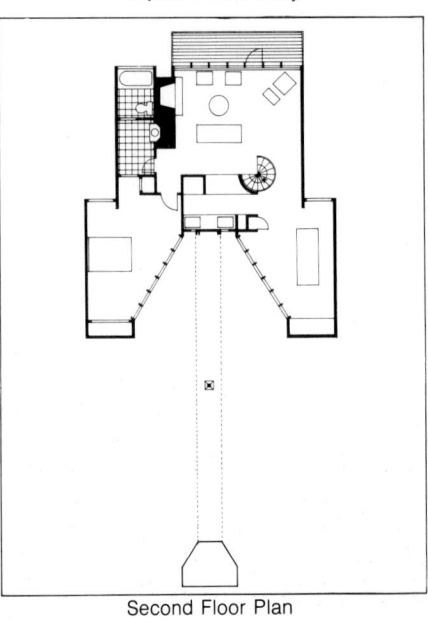

Second Floor Plan

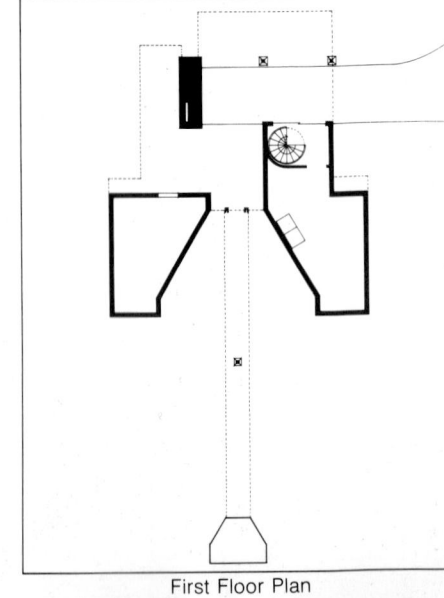

First Floor Plan

Above: View of south   Opposite: Living room with Joyce Lambeth tapestry

View of north entry

Above: View of music room   Opposite: Living room with Rosenquist

Lower bath

Above: Upper bath with prism   Below: Rainbows in upper bath

Opposite: Master bath

Belzung Residence
Fayetteville, Arkansas, 1969, Latitutde 36.03N

This residence is sited on a steep and wooded site. The single loaded corridor design allows all rooms to face the south and views to the valley below. The long corridor is lighted by a curved glass ceiling. The bridge entry is on axis with the stairway and focuses, upon entry, on a large tree. The transverse axis of the corridor bridges across the living room and is ended with mirrors.

Perspective of entry and living room

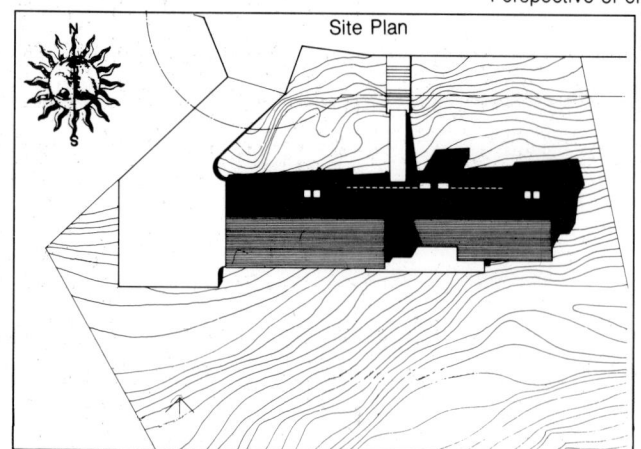
Site Plan

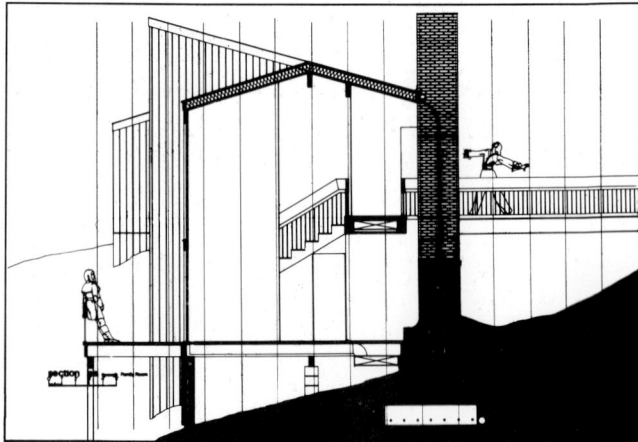

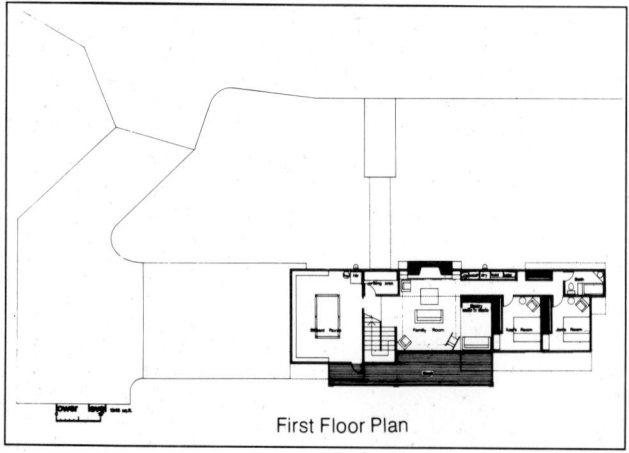
First Floor Plan

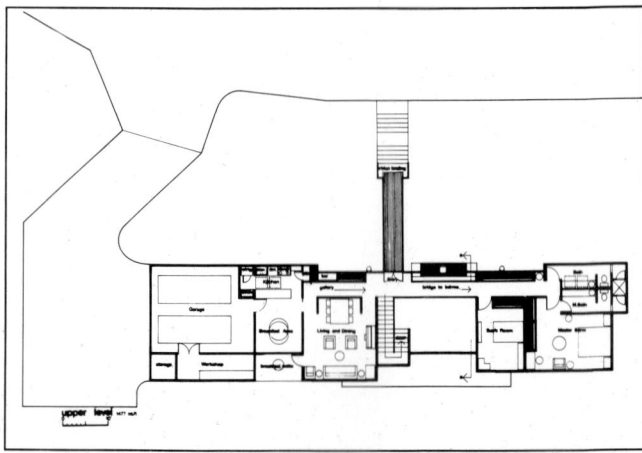

Following Page: North entry

Lushbaugh Lake House
Beaver Lake, Arkansas, 1970, Latitude 36.09N

Southwest view

Southeast view

"Taking maximum advantage of the lakeside site, all rooms feature a view of the water. Entry to the house is on the upper level, from the side opposite the lake.

A gallery stretching the entire width of the house connects the three bedrooms on the upper level. The two children's bedrooms are at one end of the gallery, along with a large storage closet and bath. At the opposite end is the master bedroom, which features a high, steeply sloping ceiling, and an outside balcony overlooking the lake.

Perhaps the most unusual feature of the house is the double nautical signal flag. Placed on the highest portion of the house (above the master bedroom), the brightly colored signal device is visible over much of the lake.

One exposed face of each prism is painted as one of the signal flags, while the other exposed face of each prism is painted with the design of the other signal flag. Viewed from an angle, only one side of each prism is visible and only one signal flag is seen. As the viewer moves past the house, the other flag becomes visible and the first disappears.

The two colorful signals, a blue rectangle within a white field and alternate red and yellow stripes, signify the letters S and Y respectively, each an international code flag."

Louis Joyner, SOUTHERN LIVING, 1975

Following Page: View from Beaver Lake

Combs Residence
Springdale, Arkansas, 1971, Latitude 36.06N

"This house is an application of James Lambeth's research in solar radiation as a way of heating interiors and exterior surfaces. Here, the swimming pool is placed to collect the maximum amount of solar gain in the winter and to decrease gain until mid-summer. This is done using a mirrored surface above the pool area, as the drawing (above right) indicates. The mirror is angled to the south at 75 degrees. The side walls are at 45 degrees to the south, admitting winter sunrise and sunset, and blocking off summer sunrise and sunset. This gives the Combs residence a 27 per cent gain at mid-winter, heating the water and the enclosed portion of the deck. The solar device generates powerful geometric forms, which Lambeth has used to organize his plan."
ARCHITECTURAL RECORD, 1972

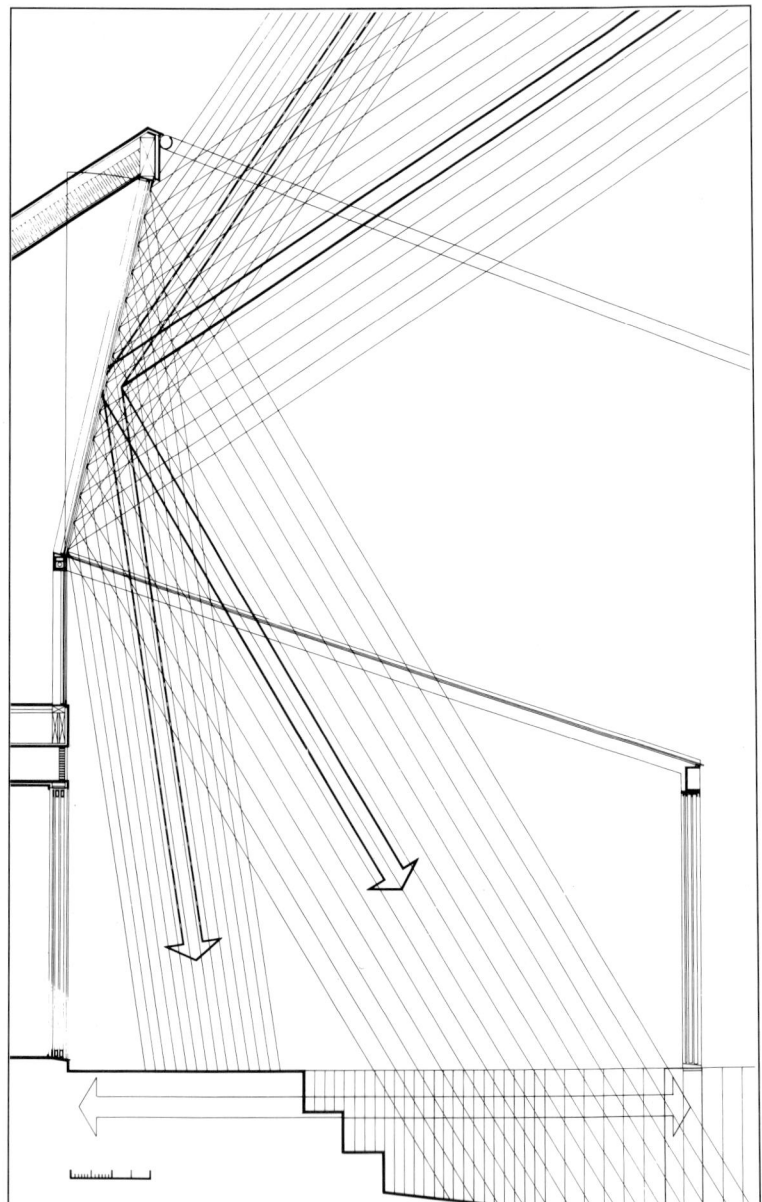

Above: Section thru lens and pool

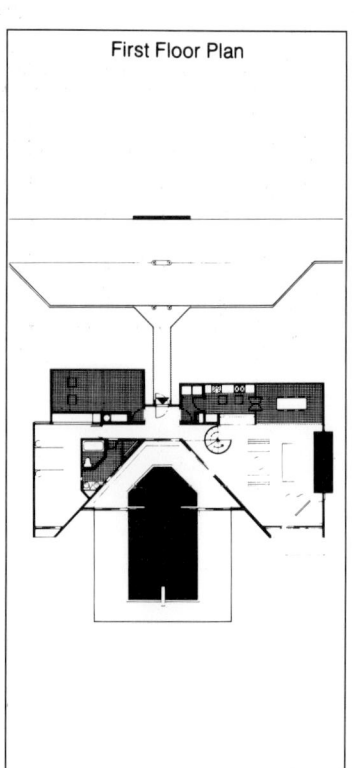

First Floor Plan

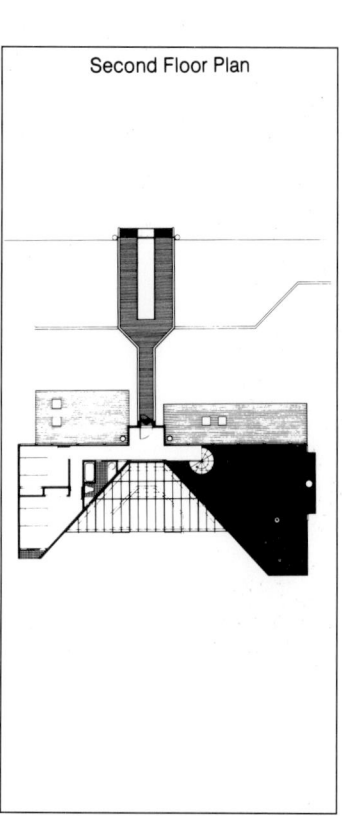

Second Floor Plan

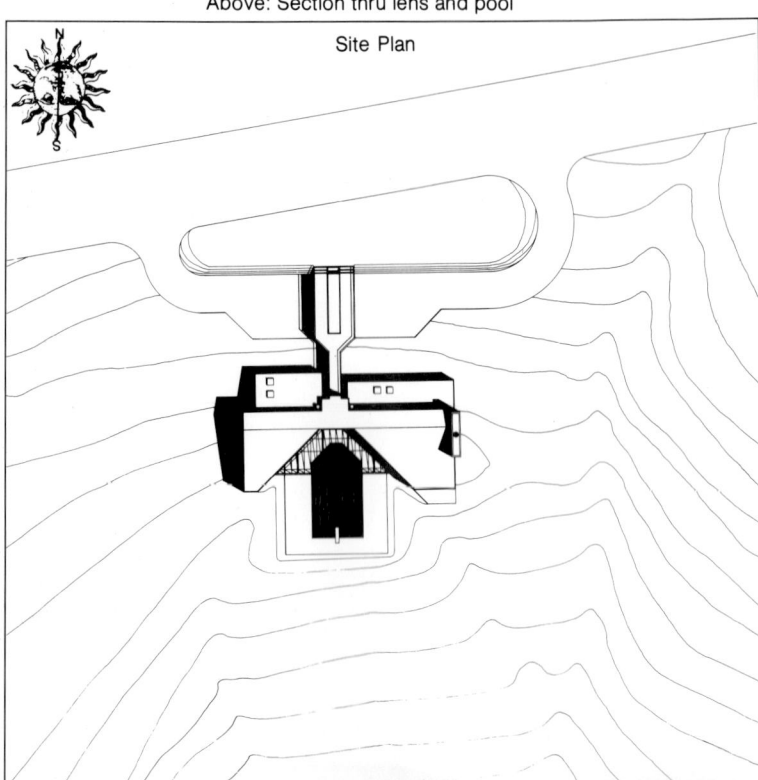

Site Plan

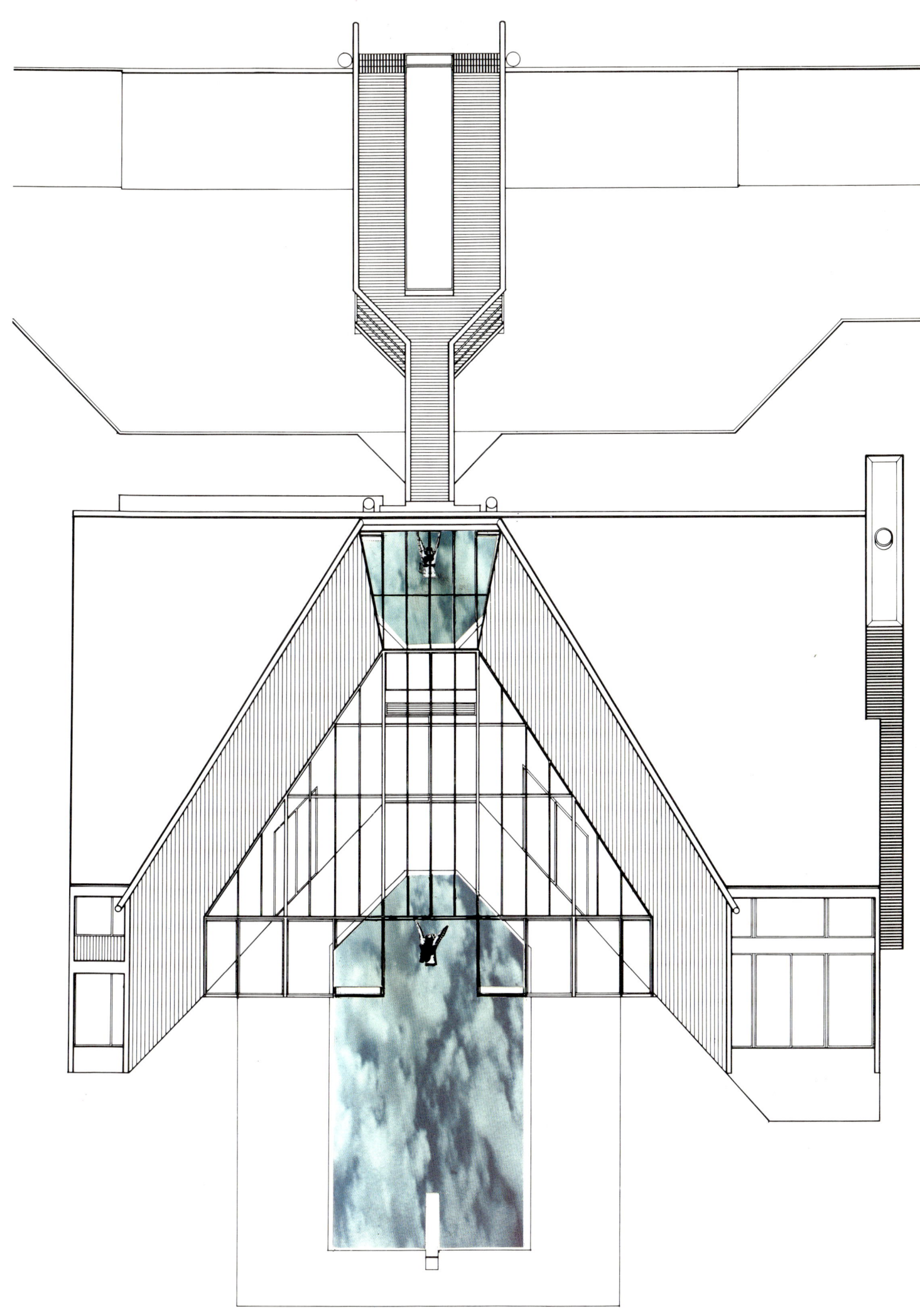

Projected plan from south

Yocum Ski Lodge
Snowmass at Aspen, Colorado, 1972, Latitude 39.12N

Above: North Elevation   Opposite: View of south elevation

"In most ways, this is a very straightforward house, a simple solution to simple needs: spaces to accommodate overnight guests and multipurpose activities. In short, a ski lodge that can take care of its owners, their guests and itself. Architect James Lambeth has used simple geometric volumes and massing to recall existing mining structures and barns in this area of Colorado. High use areas were built to withstand ski boot abuse and lounging areas provided for comfort. These considerations, plus sun deck and ample sleeping, bathing and entertaining facilities enable the house to serve many ski weekend and vacation functions.

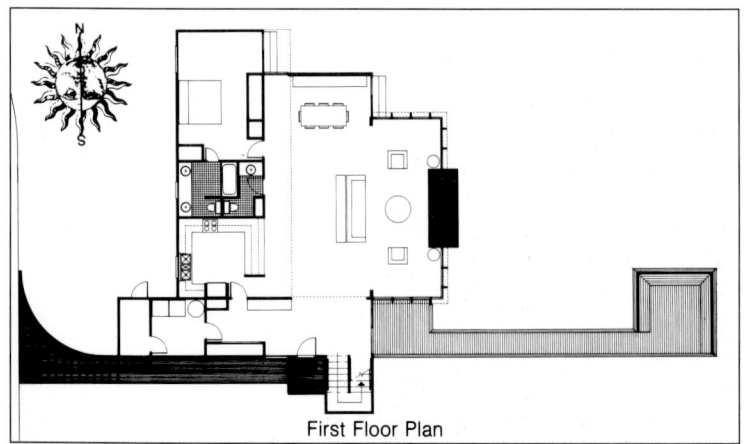

First Floor Plan

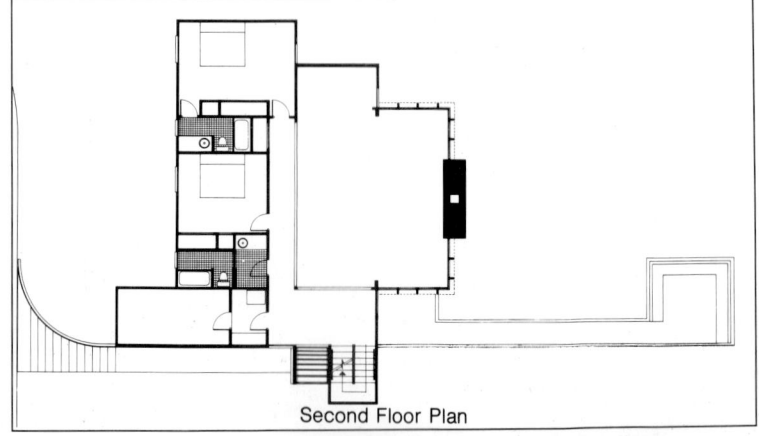

Second Floor Plan

The architect has also tried to build into the house several exterior self-maintenance features which will make life easier for occupants. Tests of prevailing north winds on study models led to the curved snow wall configuration used to protect the entrance. The realization that snow build-up near the door could not be eliminated entirely by the snow wall prompted the design of an interesting device to finish the job. Long an advocate of visual involvement of observers with the built environment (P/A, Oct. 1968, p. 174 and May 1971, p. 112), Lambeth has used reflective glass in several ways. In this house, however, its successful use as a

Above: View of south entry and reflective lens

Opposite: View of south entry

snow melting lens demonstrates a principle Lambeth intends to put to more extensive use. "It was found that a mirror glass surface of 80 percent reflectivity could produce a heat gain of 40 to 45 degrees at the focus plane. The lens works as planned. It feels like an electric heater high above your head. The snow is not only melted, but is vaporized," says the architect. Plotted to collect incident sun and reflect it on a given focal path from September through March, the lens is an initial, if small, demonstration of energy conservation. Its application to winter heating on a large scale is being studied."

James A. Murphy, PROGRESSIVE ARCHITECTURE, 1972

Above: View of the west side   Opposite: Reflective lens and Snowmass valley

Snow melting lens engaged   Construction section of lens

Above: Ski rack   Opposite: Reflective lens detail

38

Interior with tapestry by Joyce Lambeth

Deck extending to the east

"God bless America"

"The Sundance Kids"

"Ski Warm-up"

Solar Lens Fantasy
1972

"We of Domus immediately liked James Lambeth's projects on the use of solar lenses, for two reasons: his idea of creating 'micro-climates' from a domestic to a 'geographical' scale, and his idea of making the 'architectural object' disappear in the (reflected) landscape. We like his realizations and his visions."
Lisa Licitra Ponti, DOMUS, 1972

"Sun-catcher"

McKamey Residence
Fayetteville, Arkansas, 1973, Latitude 36.03N

"The polished mirror facade of this Ozark Mountain residence reflects the changing seasons appearing as two pieces of sky on the wooded slope. The bridge entry pierces the reflected sky and elevates the entrance into an experience or euphoria, gravity vanishes, and the sky parts.

Upon entry, the ceiling slopes downward, a skylight above a spiral stairway on the entry axis halts the movement. All windows on the downhill side view the woods and stream of the mountain site.

The east and west walls are without opening — protecting the interior from uncontrollable sunlight. Mirrors of the entry side keep private the rooms behind, sometimes partially transparent — sometimes solid. Summer sun is reflected in the glass keeping the interior cool. The winter sun enters the clear glass of the downhill walls, heating the interior during the day."
DOMUS, 1974

View of entry bridge

North Elevation

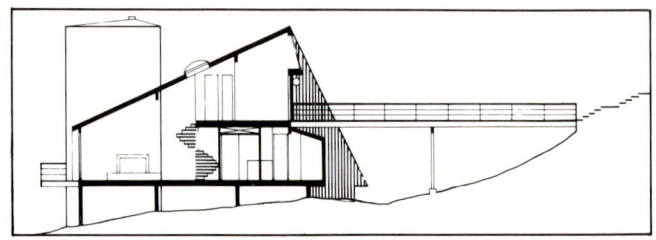
North/South Section

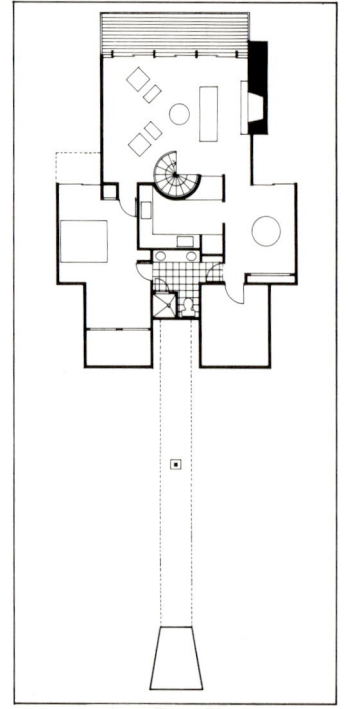
First Floor Plan

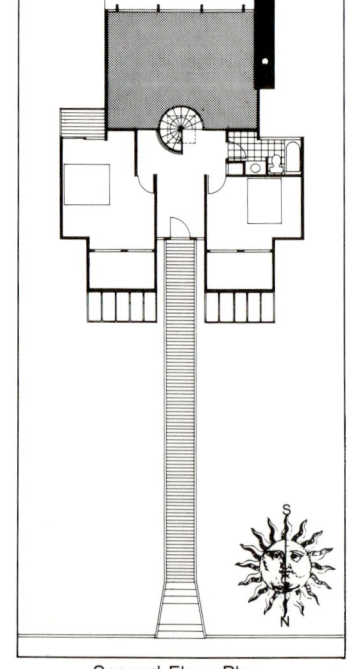
Second Floor Plan

Living Room

48

Dewar's Profile
1978

Layout used

Rejected layout

49

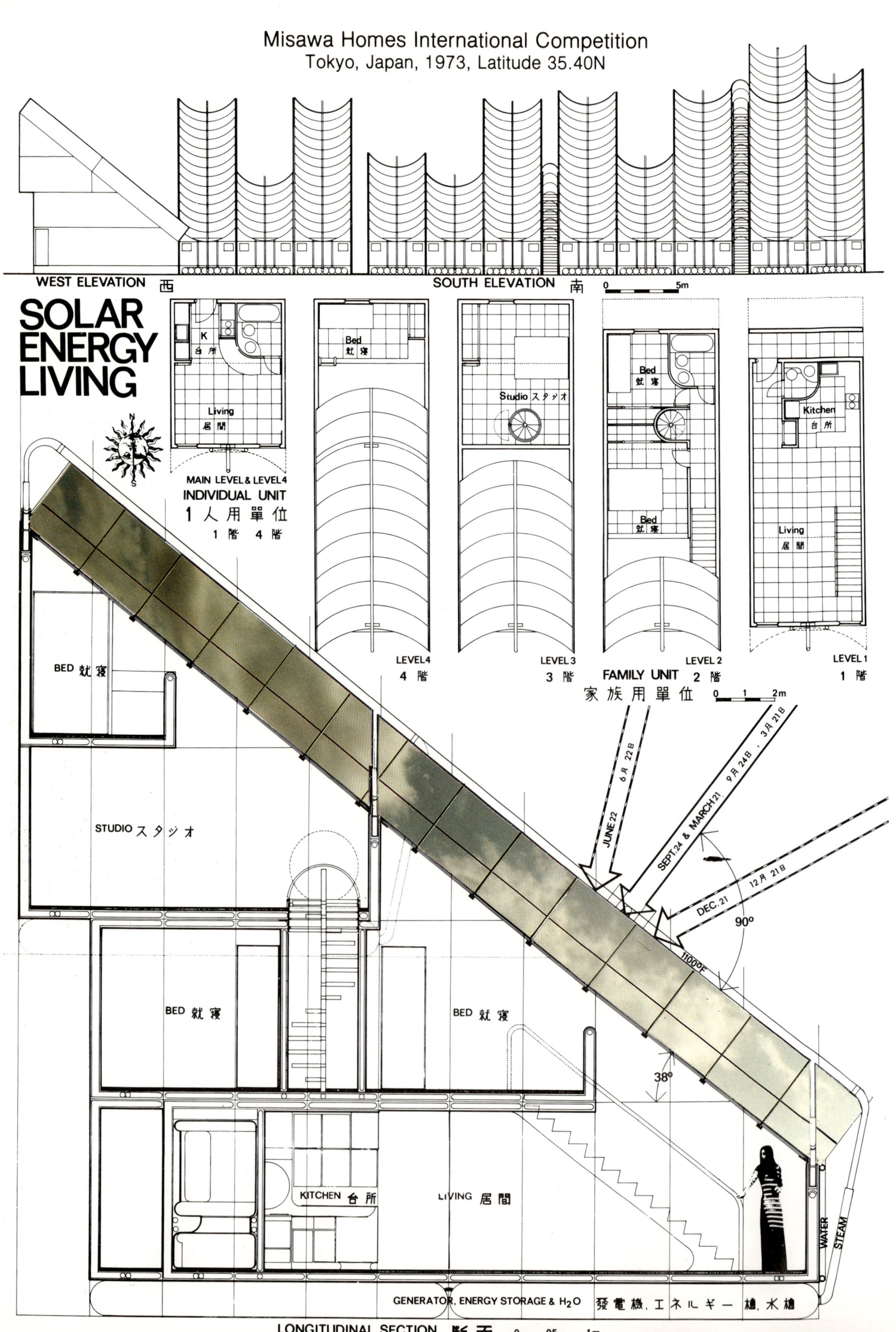

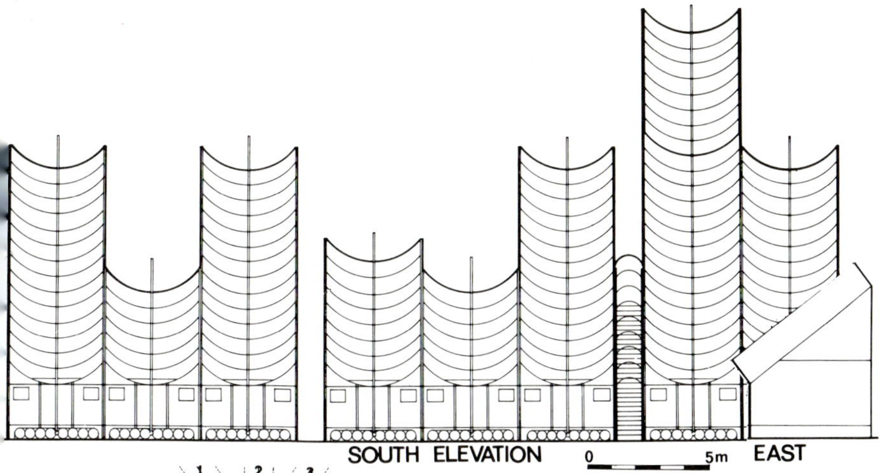

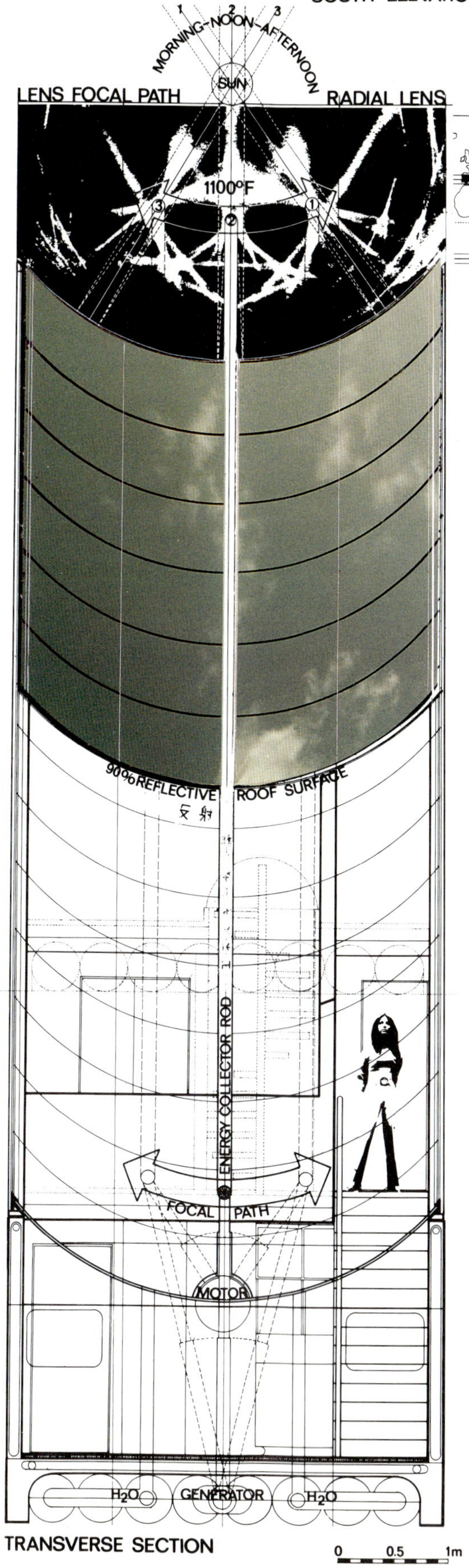

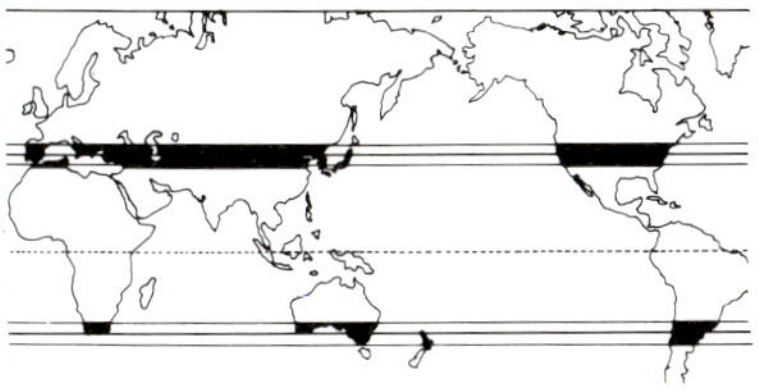

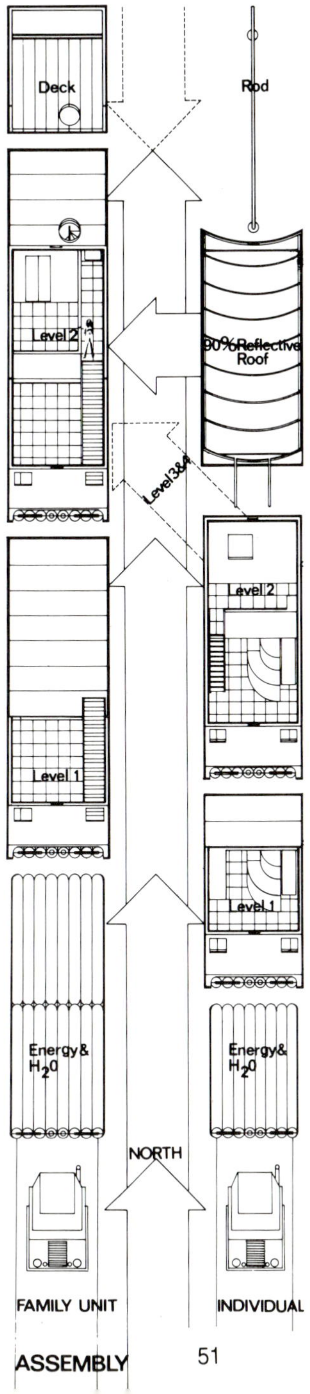

South view

"The Solar Energy Living project shows an architecture shaped by the directional relationship of sun to earth.

A reflective lens-roof focuses solar energy onto a moving collector rod, producing app. 1.100°F.

This heat is both used directly and converted into electricity. Absorption refrigeration produces summer cooling. Storage of energy is located under the dwelling units.

The 38° angle of the lens-roof is perpendicular to the equinox and is the angle of maximum annual energy reception. The world location map shows areas of optimum use of this angle.

This system uses no more land than the units themselves. Its beauty is an integral part of its effective use of solar energy and not that of Style or Fashion."
DOMUS, 1973

Silver Necklace
1973

This necklace was designed following the Misawa Homes competition. A polished curved silver plate acts as the lens. The lineal focus of daylight is absorbed by a silver rod backed with phosphorus. At night this invisible glowing element radiates across the full face of the necklace.

Necklace in dark

Solar Module Cabin
Madison County, Arkansas, 1974, Latitude 36.50N

View of north side

With the oil embargo the problem of energy conservation became more acute. These Solar Module Cabins provided much needed data for the refinement of Passive Solar Design.

Illustrated are only two of the dozen or so cabins built throughout the mountains of Arkansas and Tennessee.

"The house you see here holds a secret. It is heated by the sun in winter and cooled by mountain breezes in summer, using no electricity or gas. And the young couple who live here have made it their year-round home for the past two years. They have been warm in winter and cool in summer.

This cabin's "secret" — efficient use of the sun — is due primarily to two things: north-south placement on its site (200 feet above the Buffalo River in Madison County, Ark.), and its unique fan shape. It was designed to be a "passive solar energy collector" by James Lambeth, A.I.A., a professor at the University of Arkansas at Fayetteville. This means that there is no mechanical collector as such. Rather, the design of the house does the "energy collecting." The house acts as its own heat storage system as well.

"If a structure is properly oriented and properly insulated, it can be from 50% to 75% efficient in collecting its winter heat from the sun," Lambeth explains.

Has this house done that? The owners, a young couple with a passion for living natural, self-sufficient life, say, "Living in this house is like a continuation of the outdoors. But it's warm in winter and cool in summer. In winter, if the weather is clear or partly cloudy outside, our house is about 45° warmer inside. So if the temperature is 30° outside, its 75° inside. As the sun sets, the interior slowly begins to cool. By morning the temperature may get as low as 50°, which we love. As the sun rises, the cycle begins again."

A small wood-burning stove is used during extremes of cold weather or when a series of overcast days has kept the sun hiding — rare in this part of the state. Very little wood is needed to heat the interior of the house comfortably.

The original Lambeth design called for a massive stone fireplace to be installed in the middle of the cabin's main living area, and for a sleeping loft above. The owners have not felt it necessary to make these additions. They may at some future time.

View of south side

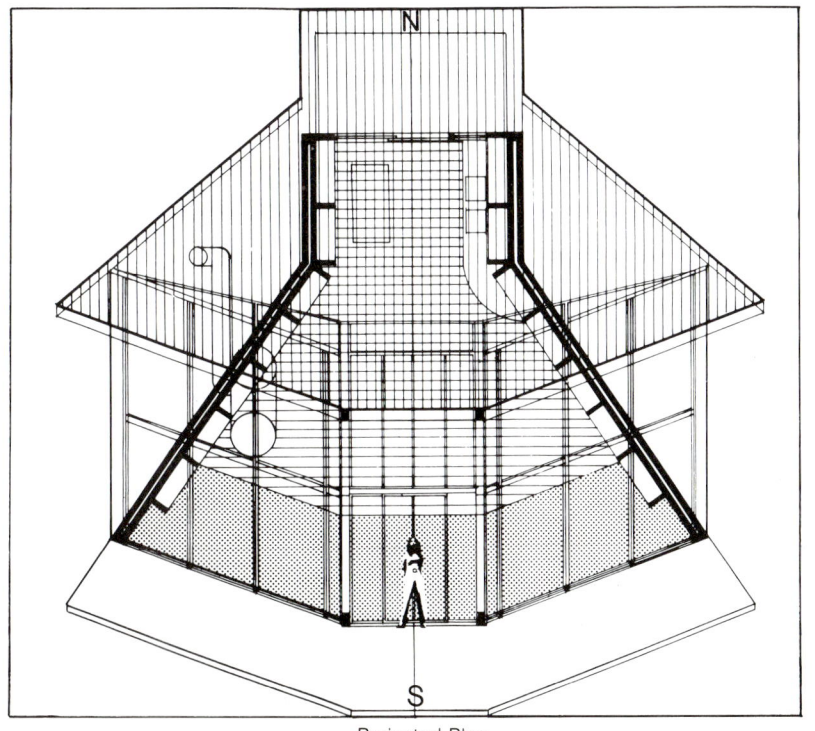
Projected Plan

Above and below: Views of interior

A 4-foot overhang along the south wall shields the interior from the direct exposure to the high summer sun, yet does not block penetration of rays of the low winter sun. In warm weather, two 8-foot-long sliding glass doors in the south wall, one atop the other, are opened in various combinations with the 8-foot-long door on the north wall. The fan shape of the house causes the breezes to sweep through in a natural air-conditioning pattern.

The roof is made of reflective aluminum which glistens in the sun. Roof and east and west walls, which have no openings, are well insulated. Interior walls, which were left unfinished and all their architectural details exposed so that they become a part of the decor, act as additional insulation.

Vegetable and fruit storage is underground with access through a trap-door located in the kitchen area. Stone-lined, it remains a constant 50° F. year round.

Just as it works for people, the solar environment works well for plants, fruits, and vegetables grown indoors in starter pots and flats during the winter.

This energysaving solar house should, according to Lambeth, function equally as well some 50 years from now as it does today because there is nothing to wear out. Imagine how much more comfortable our pioneer ancestors could have been if they had had access to large amounts of glass."
Felicia Butsch, PROGRESSIVE FARMER, 1977

Solar Module Cabin
Washington County, Arkansas, 1974, Latitude 36.28N

View of north entry

Above: Interior

Opposite: View of south from below

Hinged wall closed

Hinged wall open

The Washington County design has twenty foot hinged walls on the south corners of the structure. These are insulated and covered with mirrors on the inner surface.

During the summer and long periods of sunless days, the walls are closed to protect the interior. During sunny winter days the walls are opened to reflect additional solar radiation into the interior stone thermal storage walls inside the cabin.

Wall detail

Solar Module Cabin
Working Drawings

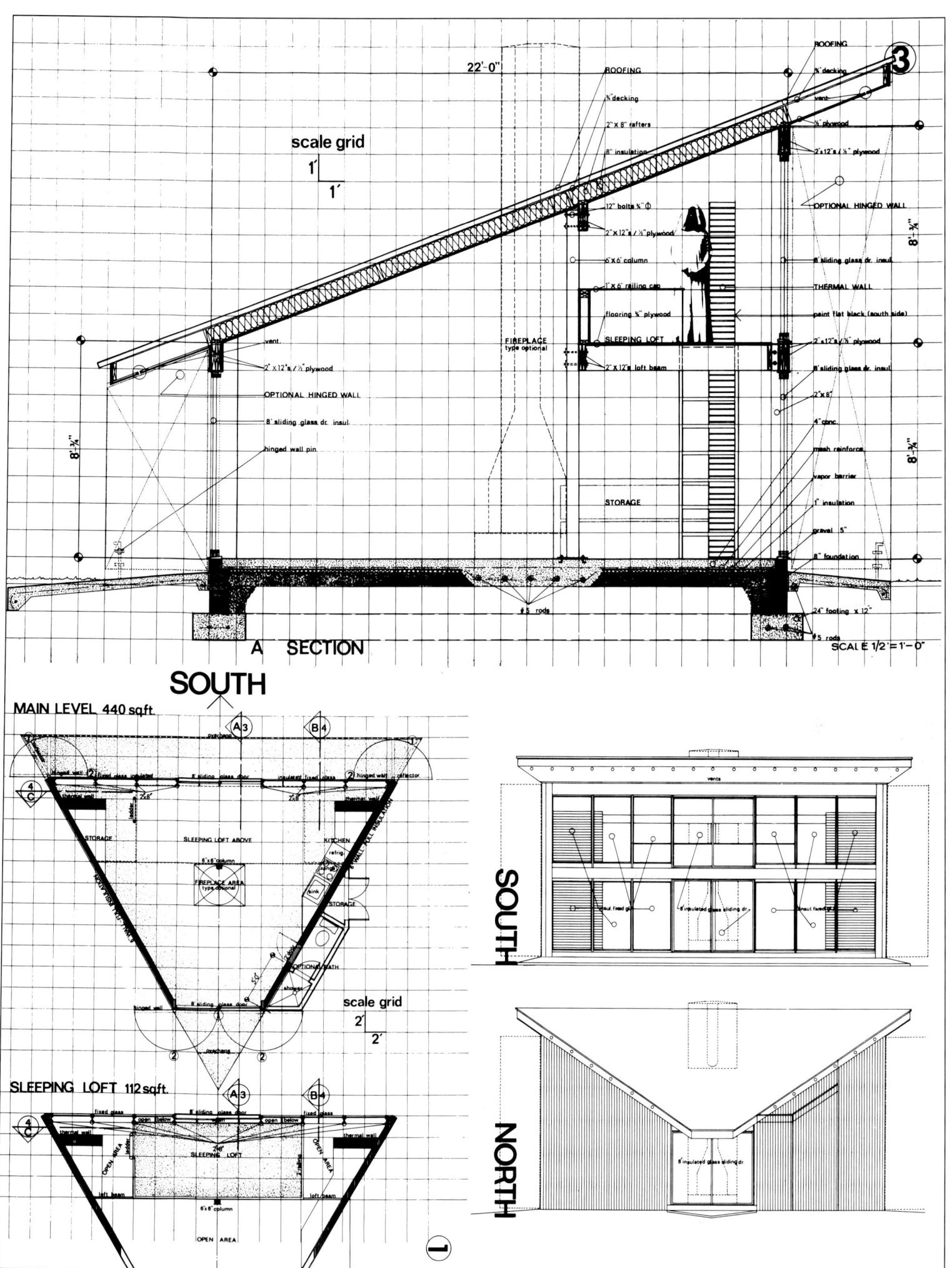

Strawberry Fields Apartments East
Springfield, Missouri, 1974, Latitude 37.11N

Approaching apartments and pool from the south

The three-story structure of this apartment ends on the south with the swimming pool. This is the first time Lambeth was able to combine his lens development with collectors to heat water. This stainless steel lens is constructed to reflect added energy to the collector system during the spring and fall. The collectors are shaded in mid-summer.

Visually, the lens reflects and abstracts the colors and activities of the pool area.

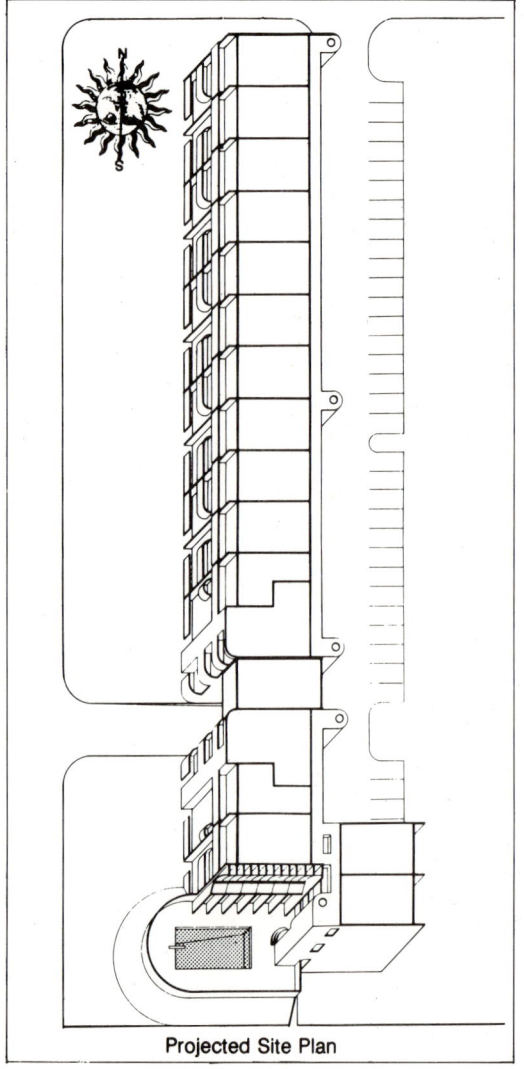
Projected Site Plan

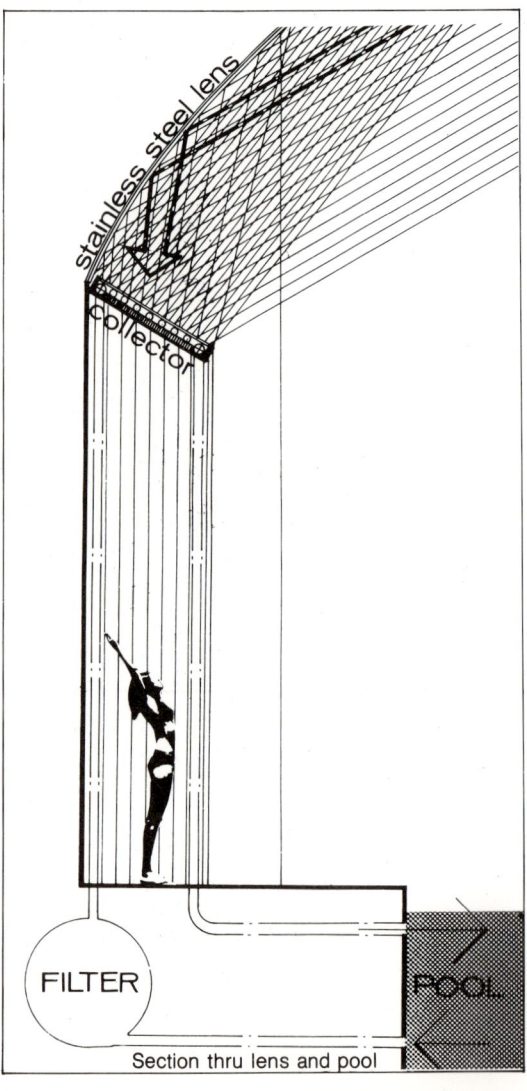
Section thru lens and pool

Focusing lens and collectors

Swimming pool

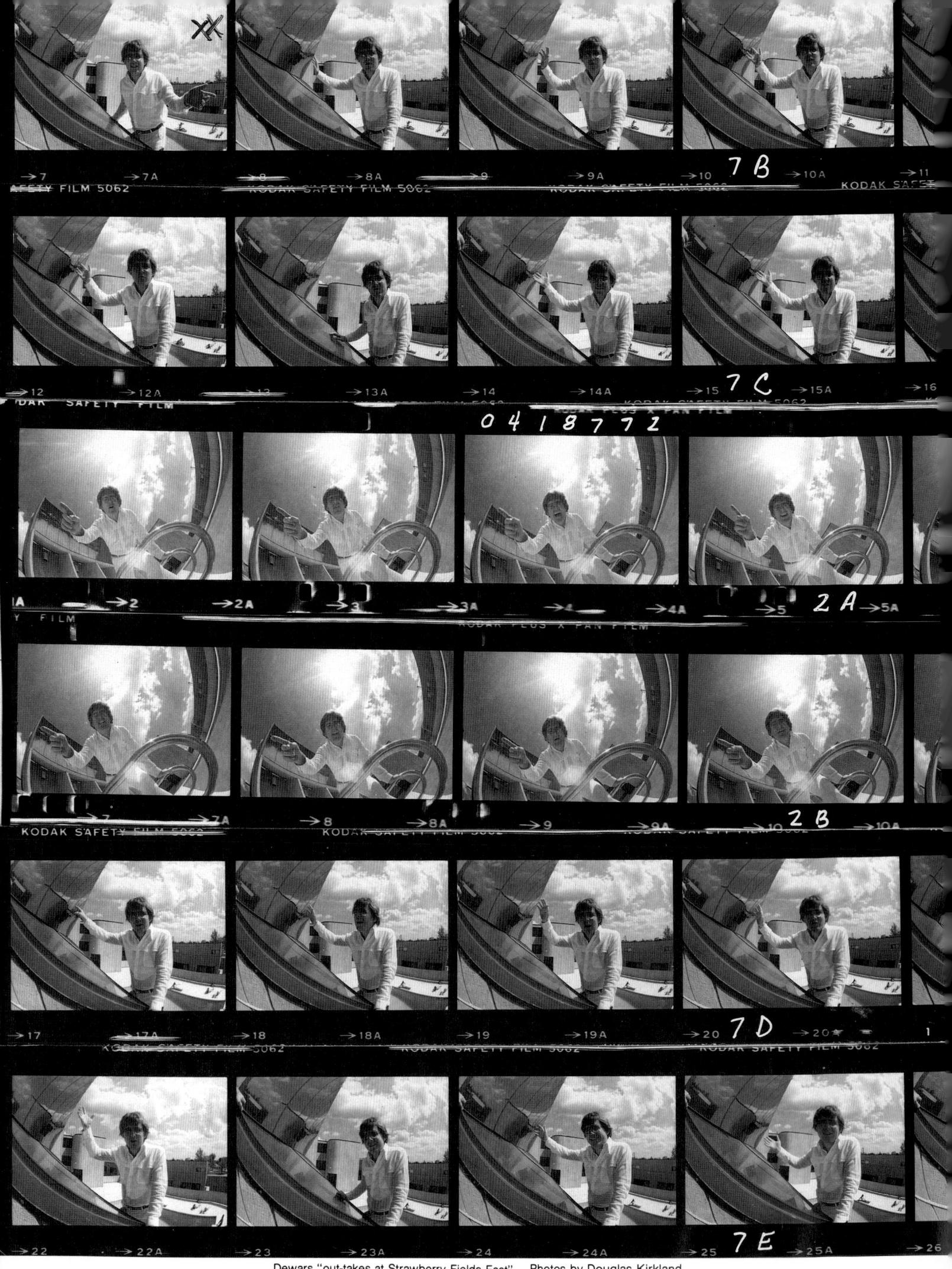

Dewars "out-takes at Strawberry Fields East"   Photos by Douglas Kirkland

Reflective lens

Architectural Design of Great Britain responded to this project by giving it the "worst utilization of energy technology" in 75 Others to receive the award were NASA, Union Carbide, and Mother Earth News.

"Not quite so nasty, but hotly contended, are the Property Speculator's Cash-In-On-The-Publicity Stakes. A forerunner award goes to the builders of the solar-heated pool of the Strawberry Fields Apartments, for their speed off the mark, and for the name, so alluring to Beatle-era young-executive grooviles."
ARCHITECTURAL DESIGN, 1975

Strawberry Fields Apartments also won the "Excellence in Engineering Award" by the American Iron and Steel Institute the same year.

Delap Residence
Fayetteville, Arkansas, 1974, Latitude 36.03N

View from the air

"Based on lessons learned in the design of a nearby one-room mountain cabin, this three bedroom, two bath passive solar house for a teacher and his family was built in the forested hills near Fayetteville. Its whimsical "Mickey Mouse" driveway (cars park on the ears) was designed in honor of a newborn son.

Drawings of the Delap house demonstrate the energy conscious aspects of the design. The southern elevation is open to winter sun and protected from summer sun by an overhanging roof. At the same time, the canted east and west walls open the house's interior to both sun and view."

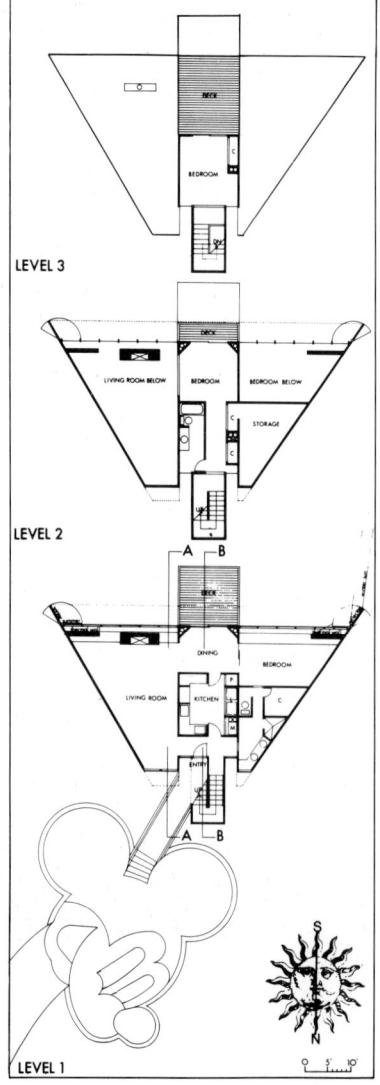
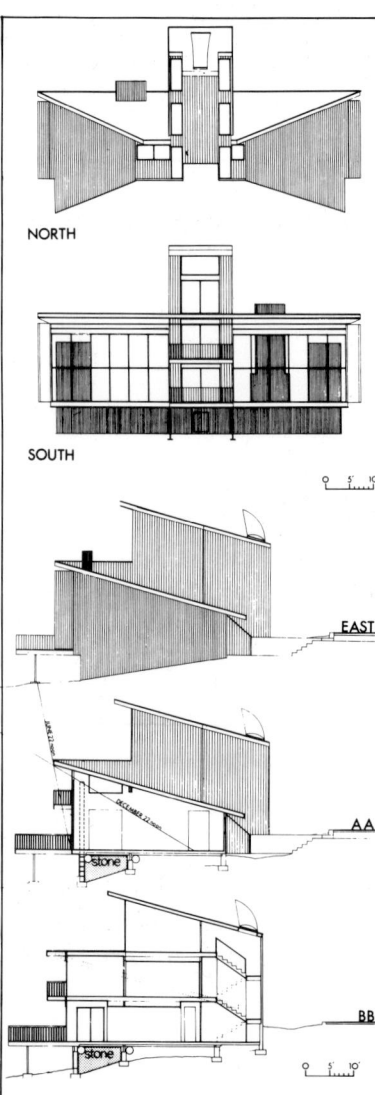

View of north side of home

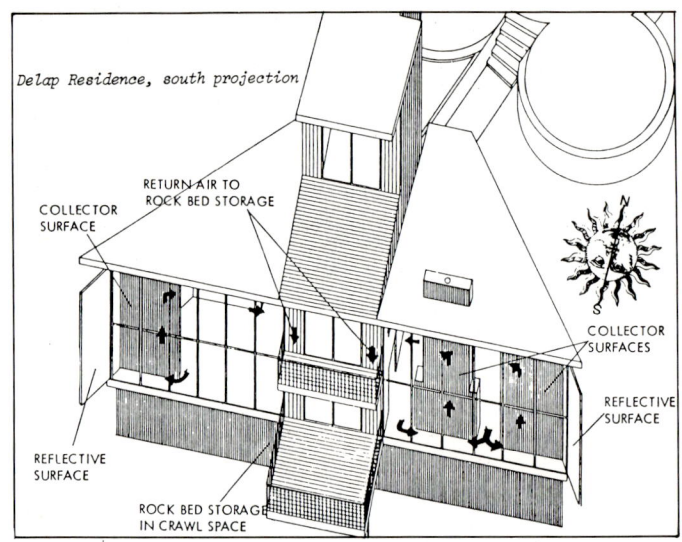

Thermal flow diagram

Passive designs accept and store solar energy in winter and shade themselves in summer. The form of passive structures tells all about how they work. As they respond directly to earth-sun relationships, they are, in effect, solar compasses and solar timepieces — giving direction, season and time of day. In this house, thermal energy is stored in painted black masonry walls on the interior of south-facing windows, and also below the floor in a stone-filled chamber of the return air duct.

In a recent survey of solar houses by the National Science Foundation, the Delap residence was one of the three most successful, economically and technically. Investment in the solar application will be recovered in less than eight years. Its technical sophistication is the result of intelligent siting, choice of materials and construction methods and integrative design skills that produced a building that truly works with the environment.

Marguerite Villecco, DESIGN QUARTERLY, 1977

View of dining room

Living room from master bedroom

Living room looking south

View toward the south from lower bedroom

South Elevation

Solar Village
Lake of the Ozarks, Missouri, 1975, Latitude 38.02N

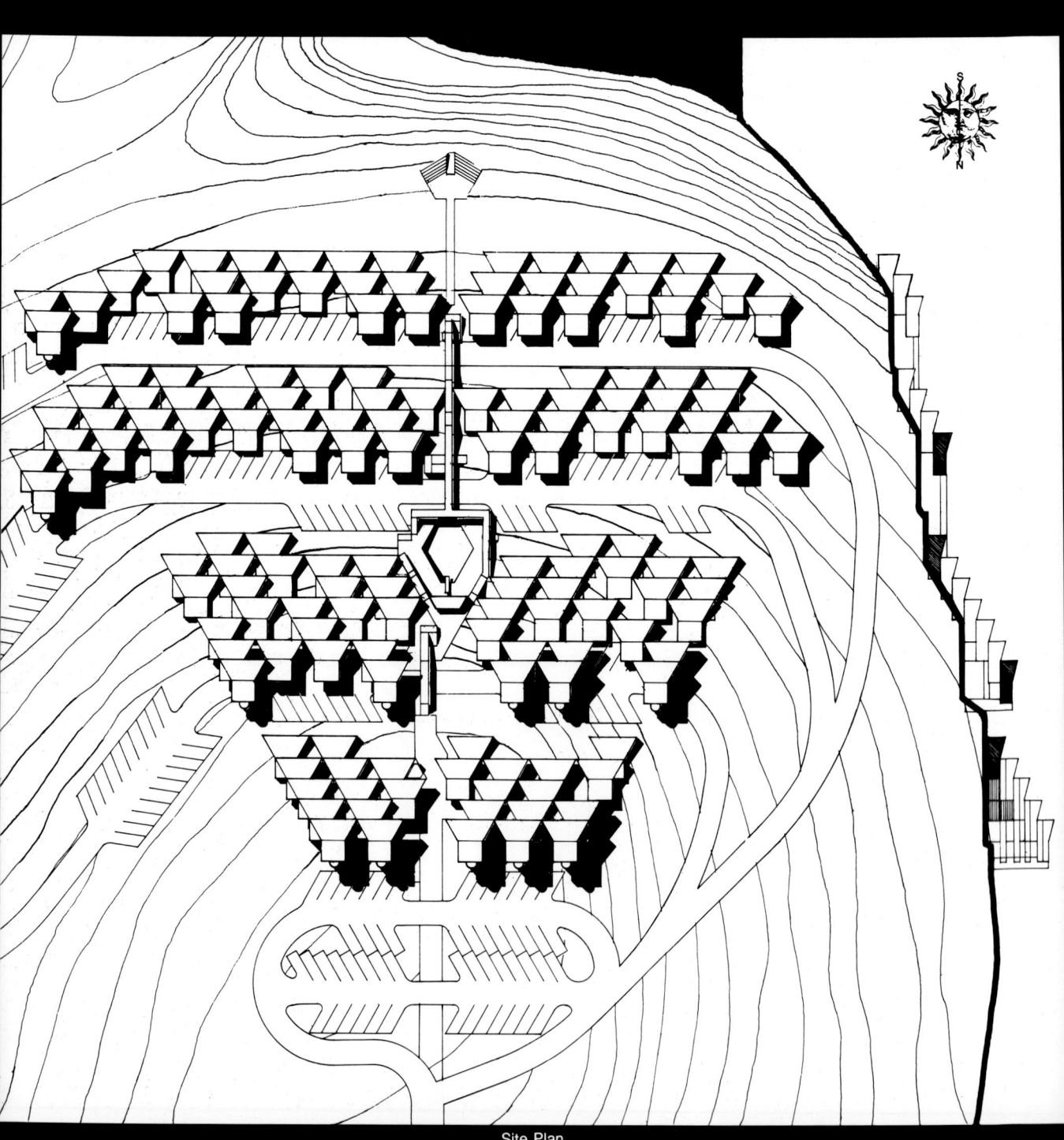

Site Plan

"The recreational community design was the result of studies in solar efficient forms. A unit module was developed that supplied 75% of its internal climate control without any mechanical devices (passive solar system). A combination of large amounts Of insulated glass and limited interior volume produced the form. Additional protection from summer sun is provided by large overhangs. The solar module was then studied in terms of different geometric groupings, always following strict rules concerning southern glass exposure.

The best grouping cascading down the southern slope to the lake provides each unit with a view of the mountain from private decks and a clear view over the module in front. In this way low winter sun penetration through the large glass wall of each structure is unobstructed. Parking, access, and service are from below. The plug-in, leave-out modular grid permits trees and light to permeate the village texture."

Sky and Stone, UNBUILT AMERICA 1976

View of southern elevation

Transport vision

Solar Module

Hall Residence
Fayetteville, Arkansas, 1976, Latitude, 36.03N

View of west wall from the air

This site has a beautiful valley view to the west. To protect the interior from the intense summer setting sun, vertical walls are placed outside the glass. These walls block the summer setting sun but allow the winter sun into the interior.

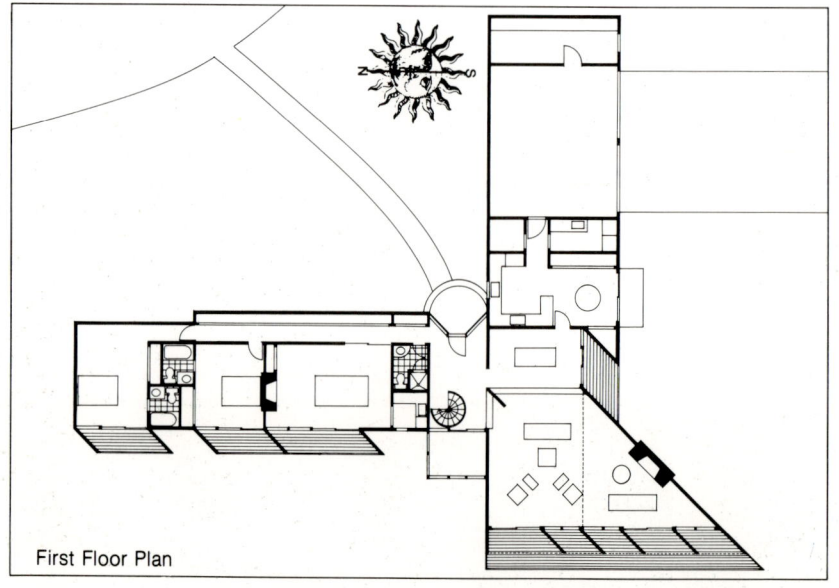
First Floor Plan

Opposite: View of entry tower

Above: View of west

Opposite: East Elevation

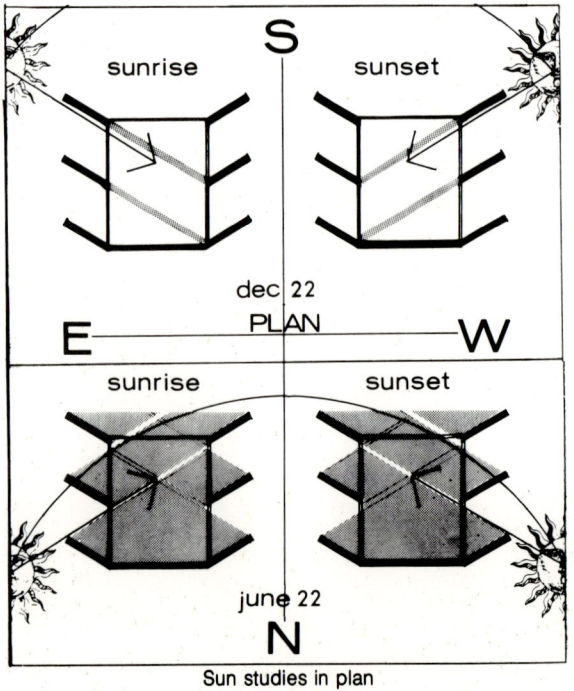

Sun studies in plan

Mobile Home Study
1976

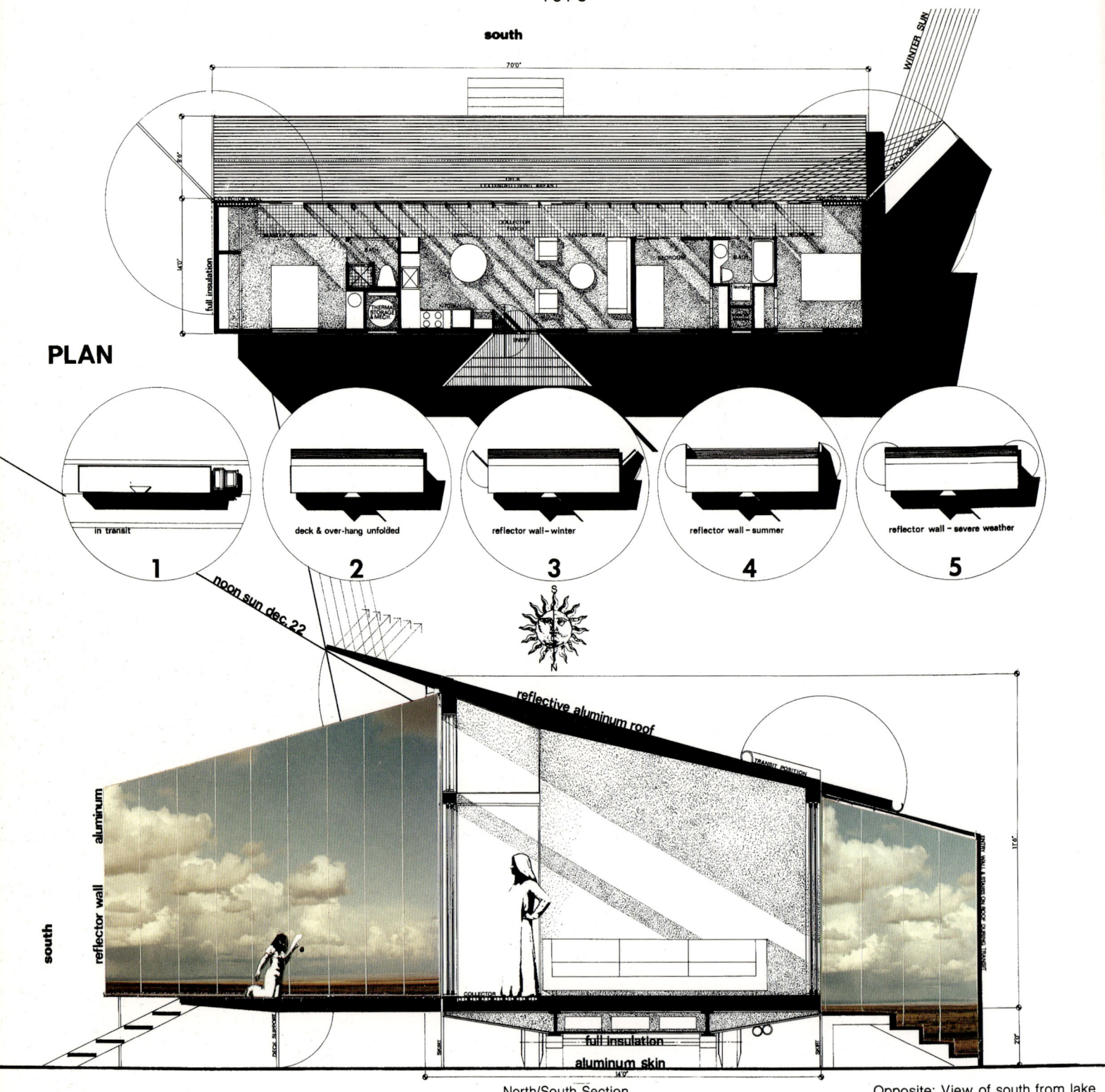

North/South Section Opposite: View of south from lake

This research project for Reynolds Aluminum, investigates the optimum form and orientation of mobile homes. Hinged walls and roof overhangs provide control of interior solar penetration. The reflective hinged end walls are conceptually the same as those on the earlier Solar Module Cabins.

Spock Residence
Beaver Lake, Arkansas, 1977, Latitude 36.10N

"When baby doctor and political activist Benjamin Spock and his wife moved to the Ozark Mountains of Arkansas, they chose a lakeside site where the veteran sailor could both see and be on the water.

Architect James Lambeth responded by designing the southern elevation of the Spocks' new home to consist solely of eight-by-eight-foot sliding glass doors, offering an unbroken view of the water and allowing maximum penetration of sunlight in the winter months. The heat from that direct solar gain is stored in interior concrete walls and a foot-thick slab floor that total 700 cubic feet of thermal massing.

Benjamin Spock in living room

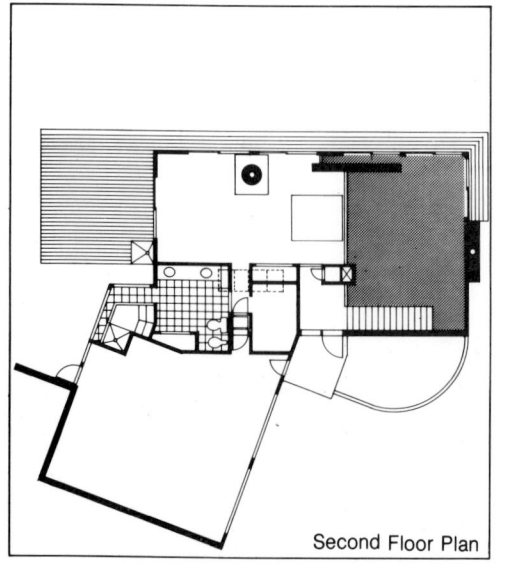

Second Floor Plan

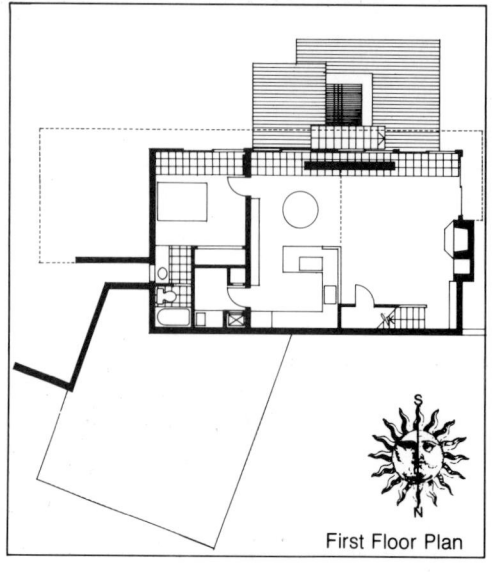

First Floor Plan

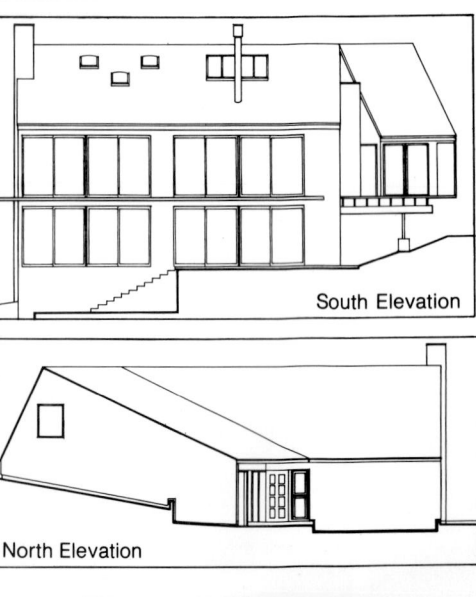

South Elevation

North Elevation

All rooms in the 2,000-sf house open to decks or patios, and a three-foot catwalk wraps the house on its south and west sides. Together with an overhanging roof, those elements shade the house from the high summer sun and ease a cooling load already minimized through natural ventilation.

A 48-sf flat-plate solar collector provides for most of the Spocks' domestic hot water needs. A forced-air electric heat pump backs up the designer's passive space heating and cooling techniques. But the home's renowned residents say the first winter's utility bills have yet to rise above $30 a month.''
RESEARCH AND DESIGN, 1979

Lake view of dock and home

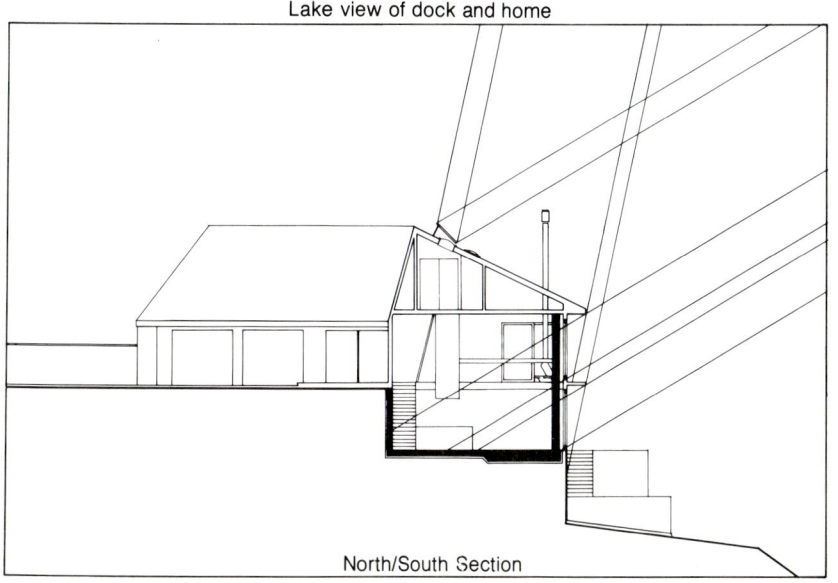

North/South Section

Strawberry Fields Apartments West
Springfield, Missouri, 1978, Latitude 37.11N

View of south elevation

This apartment complex of 110 units was placed on the back third of the gently rolling site. Two rows of buildings are served by one parking spine. In the center of the complex is the swimming pool area with laundry and office on one side. Hot water needs for the laundry and the swimming pool are supplied by the solar flat plate collectors and the connecting stainless steel solar reflector.

The one and two bedroom units are combined into two and three level buildings. All entries are served by an exterior corridor with stair towers located as needed. Each unit has an exterior deck that faces the open recreation area to the south.

Solar Pak Fantasy
1978

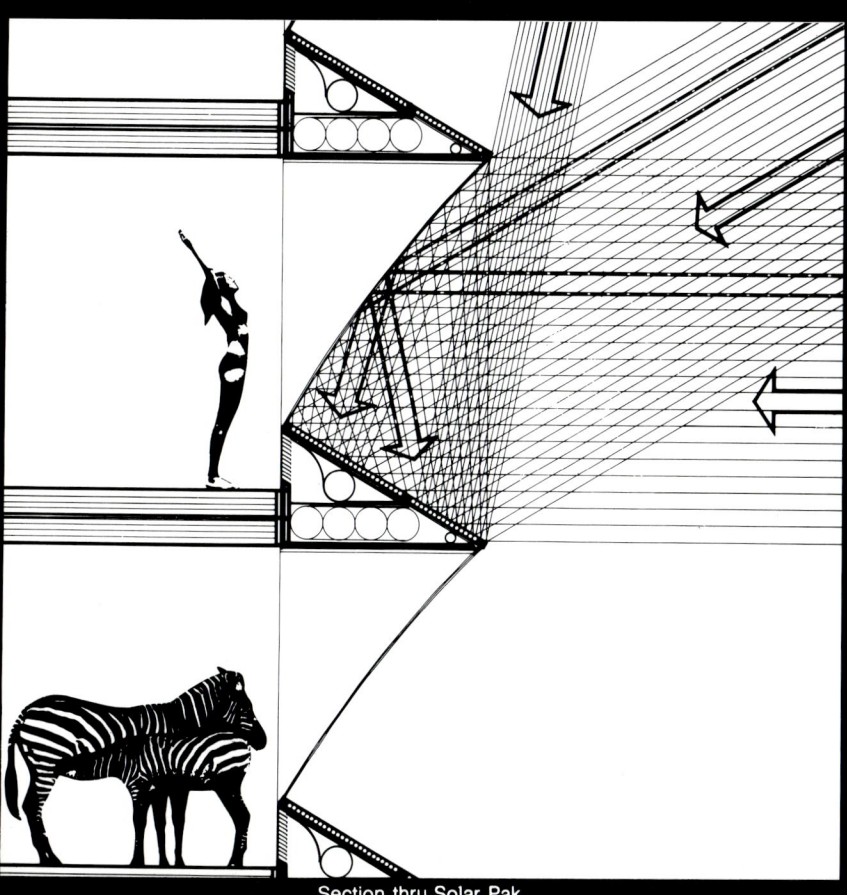

Fontainebleau Retrofit

Section thru Solar Pak.

Walker Residence
Greene County, Missouri, 1979, Latitude 37.10

Southwest view of residence

Slate fireplace in living room

"This earth sheltered residence is located in a large field and is surrounded by horses and cattle. Wind studies determined the shape of the north facade. The earth works in conjunction with the large overhang to protect the residence from cold northern winter winds. The south elevation opens to the sun. Thermal storage is provided by black slate covered concrete floors and fireplace walls.

Jorg Ludwig, SOLAR 4, 1981

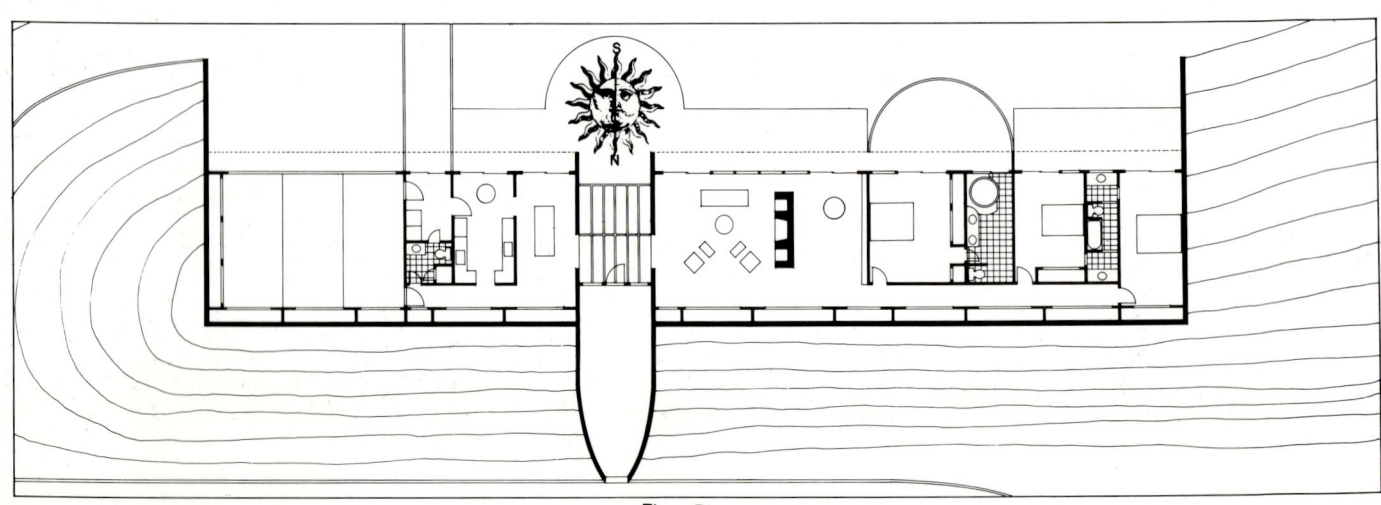
Floor Plan

View of North entry

North view of residence

Hot Springs Residence
Hot Springs, Arkansas, 1979, Latitude 34.30N

North view

View of southeast side of home

This home was designed as a middle income speculative venture for the Arkansas Department of Energy, Arkansas Power and Light, and Cooper Communities of Hot Springs, Arkansas.

The north, east, and west are earth sheltered, while the southern side is glass. Thermal storage was provided by liquid filled fiberglass tubes located inside the south glass wall.

Dixon Residence
War Eagle, Arkansas, 1979, Latitude 36.10N

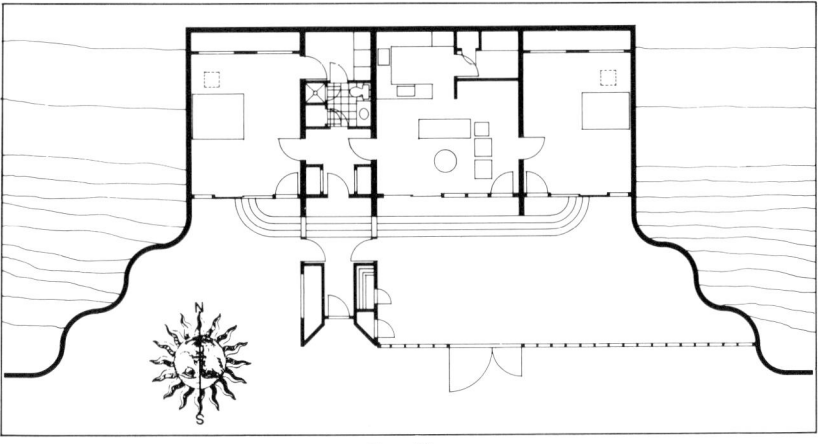

Perspective showing south entry

Floor Plan

This project was designed as a studio/residence for a stained glass artist. The simple plan incorporates earth to protect all exterior walls but the south. Thru ventilation is from operable roof skylights.

The American Academy in Rome
Rome, Italy, 1979-80, Latitude 41.53N

"The American Academy, chartered by Congress in 1905, is composed of the School of Fine Arts and the School of Classical Studies. It is a privately endowed post-graduate residential community of American artists and scholars, located in facilities atop the Janiculum Hill in Rome. Members of the community pursue independent projects in an environment structured to provide them with the time and the space to create, and the opportunity to share ideas across disciplinary lines."
AMACADMY, 1978

The Prix de Rome provided Lambeth with the time and facilities to produce the following projects of note:

The "Ma and Ra" drawings are illustrations for a children's book. The odyssey of "Ma and Ra" covers Lambeth's solar fantasies and realities of the past decade. The series was published in a limited edition of 75.

The "Sundance Paintings" show a classical solar section extrusion of building forms that react to various stimuli. Always staying in the sun, the forms are manipulated by the shadows.

Ospedale Dei Bambini
Civitavecchia, Italy, 1980, Latitude 41.55N

The Vatican requested that Lambeth study the renovation of abandoned structures by the sea for a new children's surgery hospital.

High winds from the sea blew sand into the structures. The tile and masonry walls lost heat in the winter and overheated in the summer.

Lambeth's proposal included wrapping the structure in a glass sheath. The glass, while keeping out the sand, would also trap winter solar radiation that would be transmitted to the interior. The summer heat gain would be exhausted from the skin.

View from site toward the sea

Exisiting

Retrofit

Gold Necklace
1980

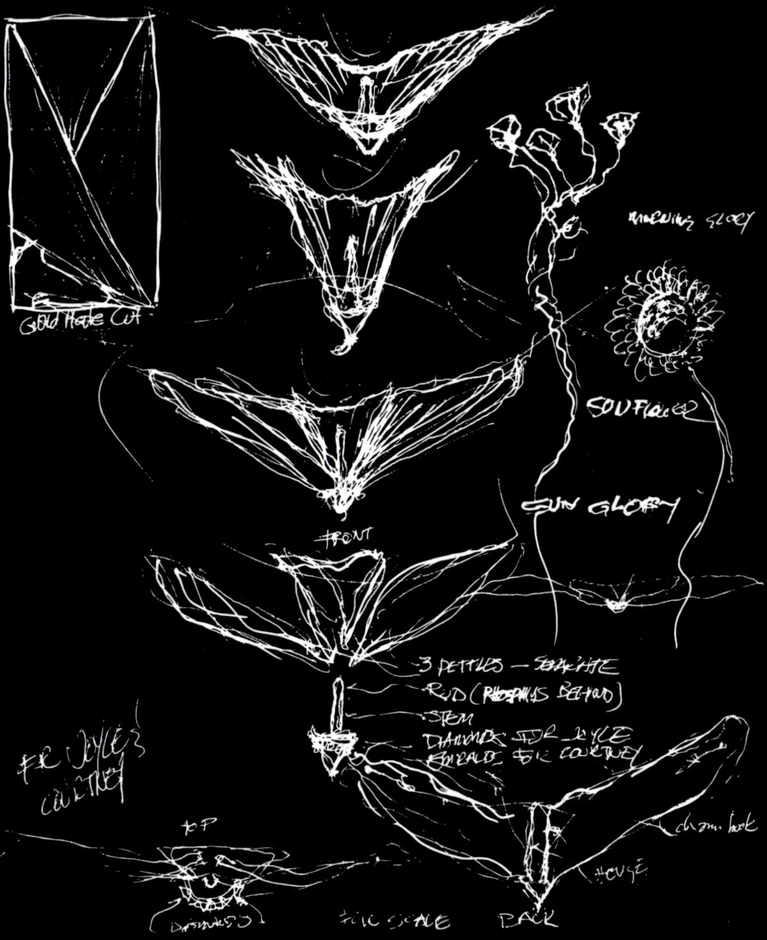

Designed for Joyce Lambeth, this necklace is a more feminine version of the silver necklace of 1973. The "flower stamen" acts as the focus receptor of the day's light. In the evening the hidden phosphorus releases its light energy across the gold petals of the necklace.

Sundance Paintings
1980

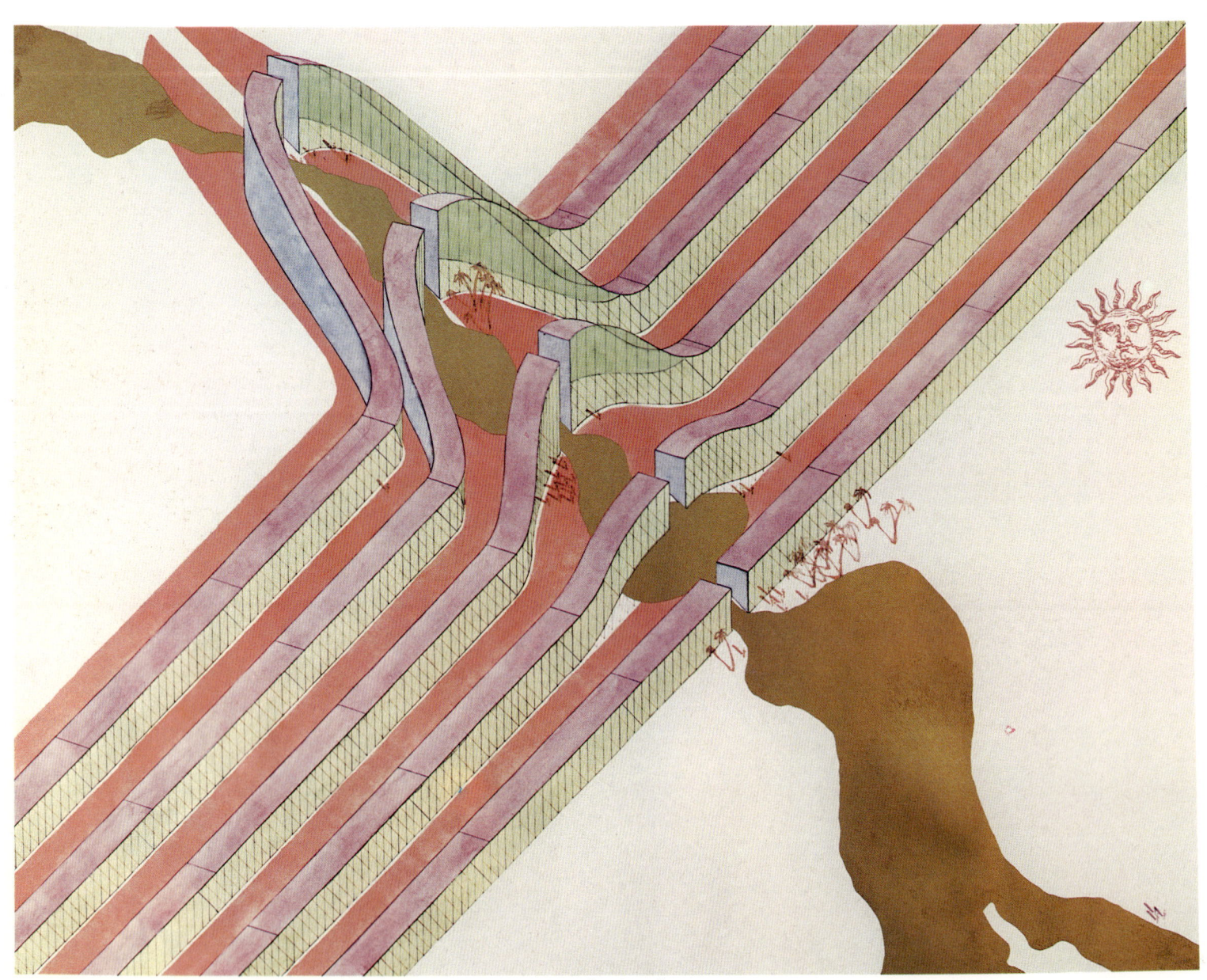

"River Sundance"

"Joyce's Sundance"

Sundance Paintings
1980

"Vineyard Sundance"

"Baptistry Sundance"

Brady Residence
Tontitown, Arkansas, 1980, Latitude 36.07N

View of entry tower

This is a residence for a car collector and his "car stables." The two linear structures create an inner courtyard. They are classical "solar section" extrusions. The southern form is penetrated by the driveway axis and the northern form is allowed to step forward in its void. This "action/reaction" of form is illustrated in his "Sundance Paintings." The entry axis culminates in a three story reflector/collector tower.

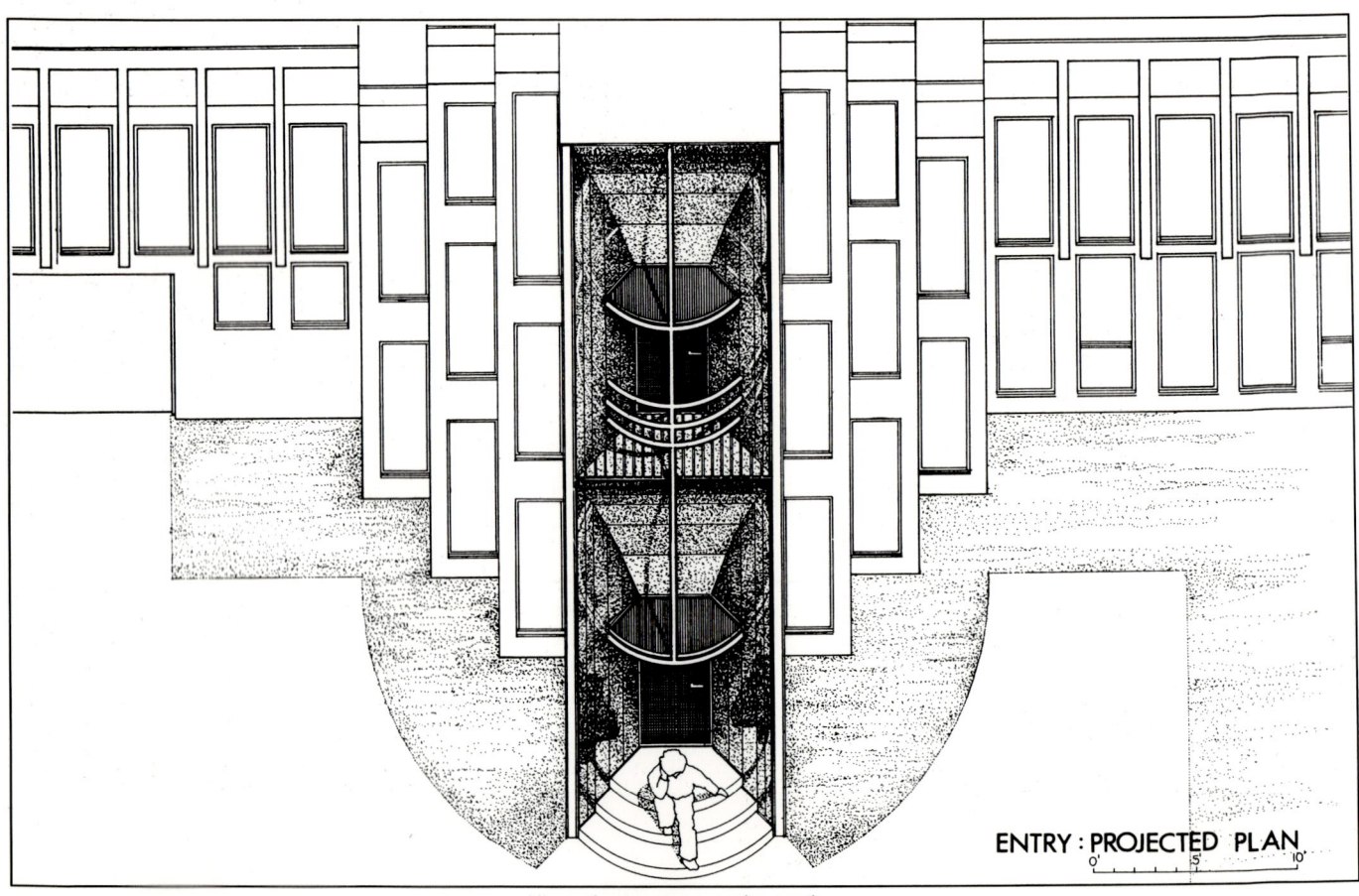
View of entry steps on the south

ENTRY: PROJECTED PLAN

Above: Views of south elevation

View of northwest

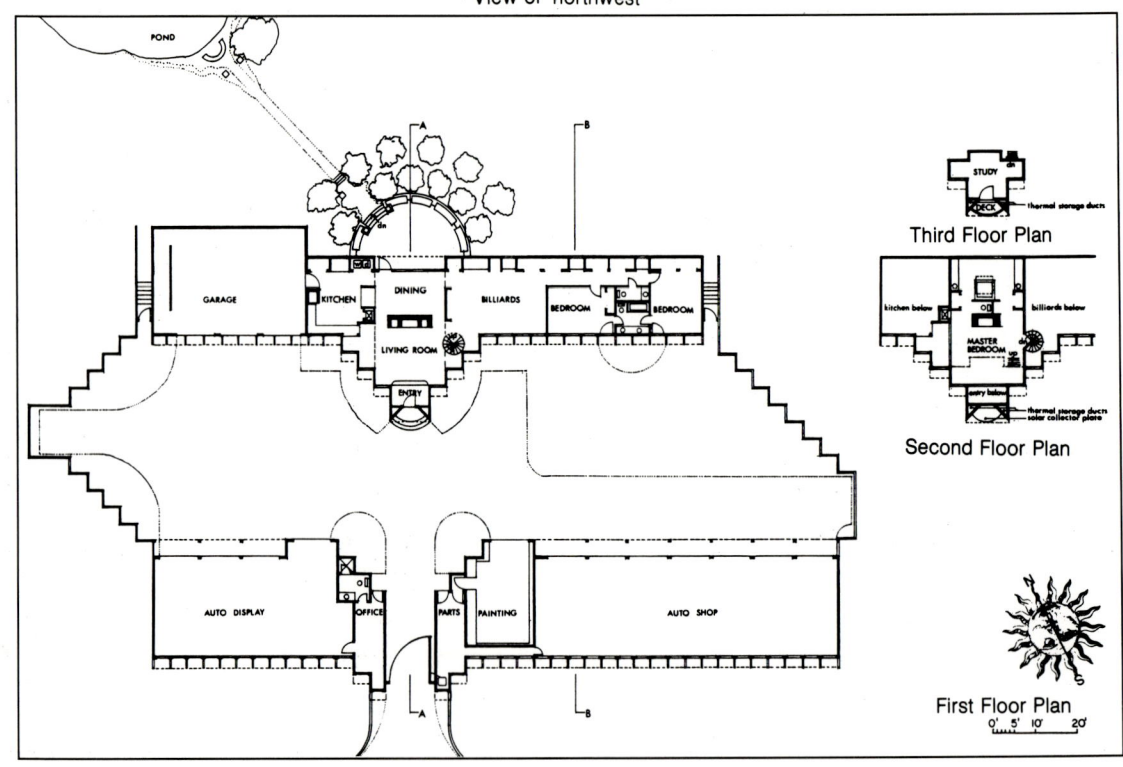

Third Floor Plan

Second Floor Plan

First Floor Plan

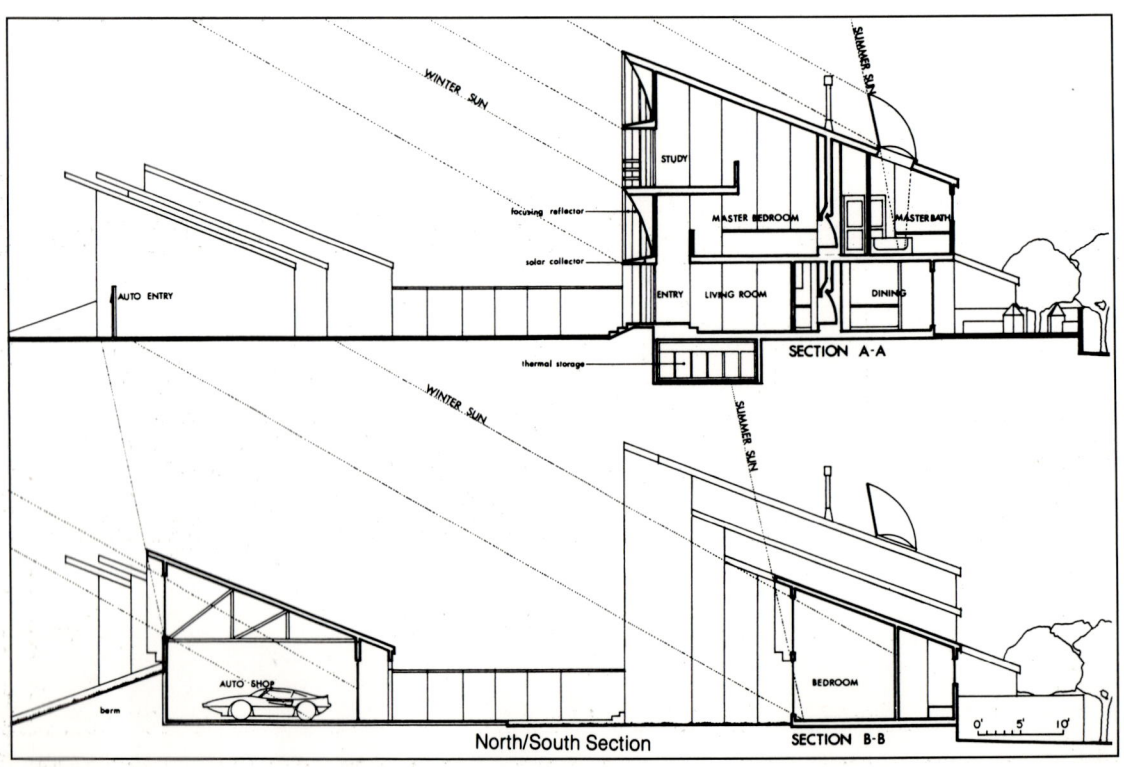

Section A-A

North/South Section

Section B-B

View of entry looking southeast

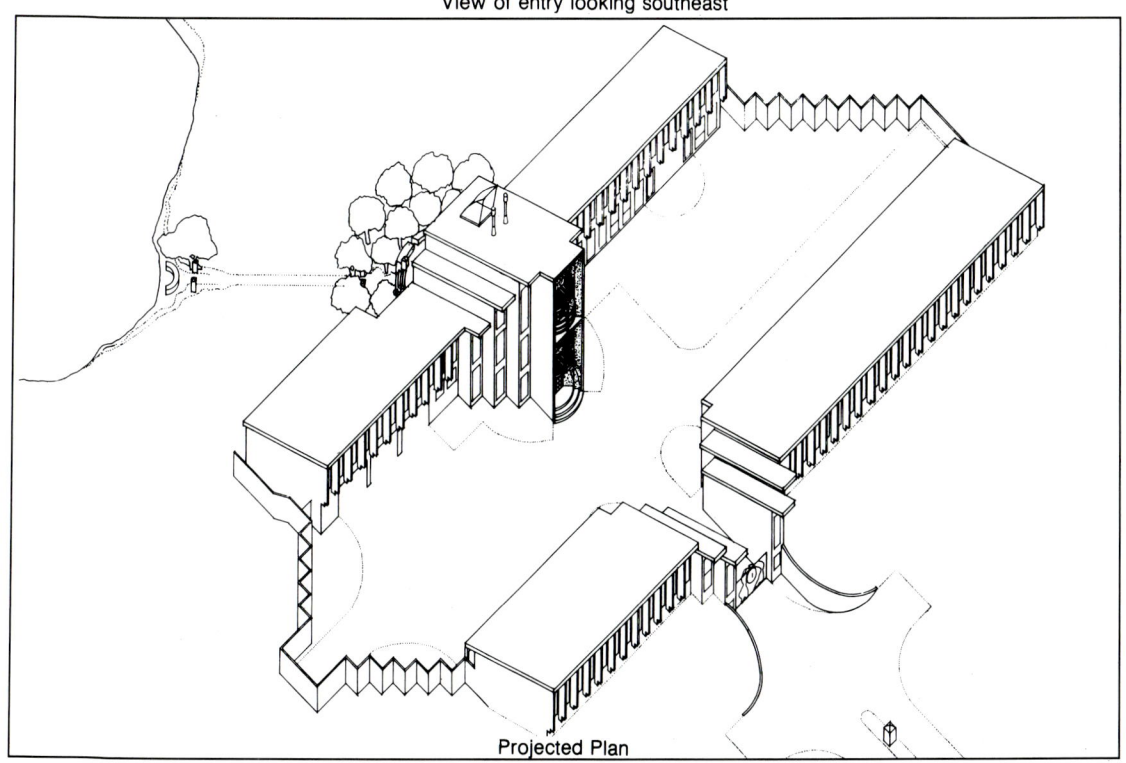
Projected Plan

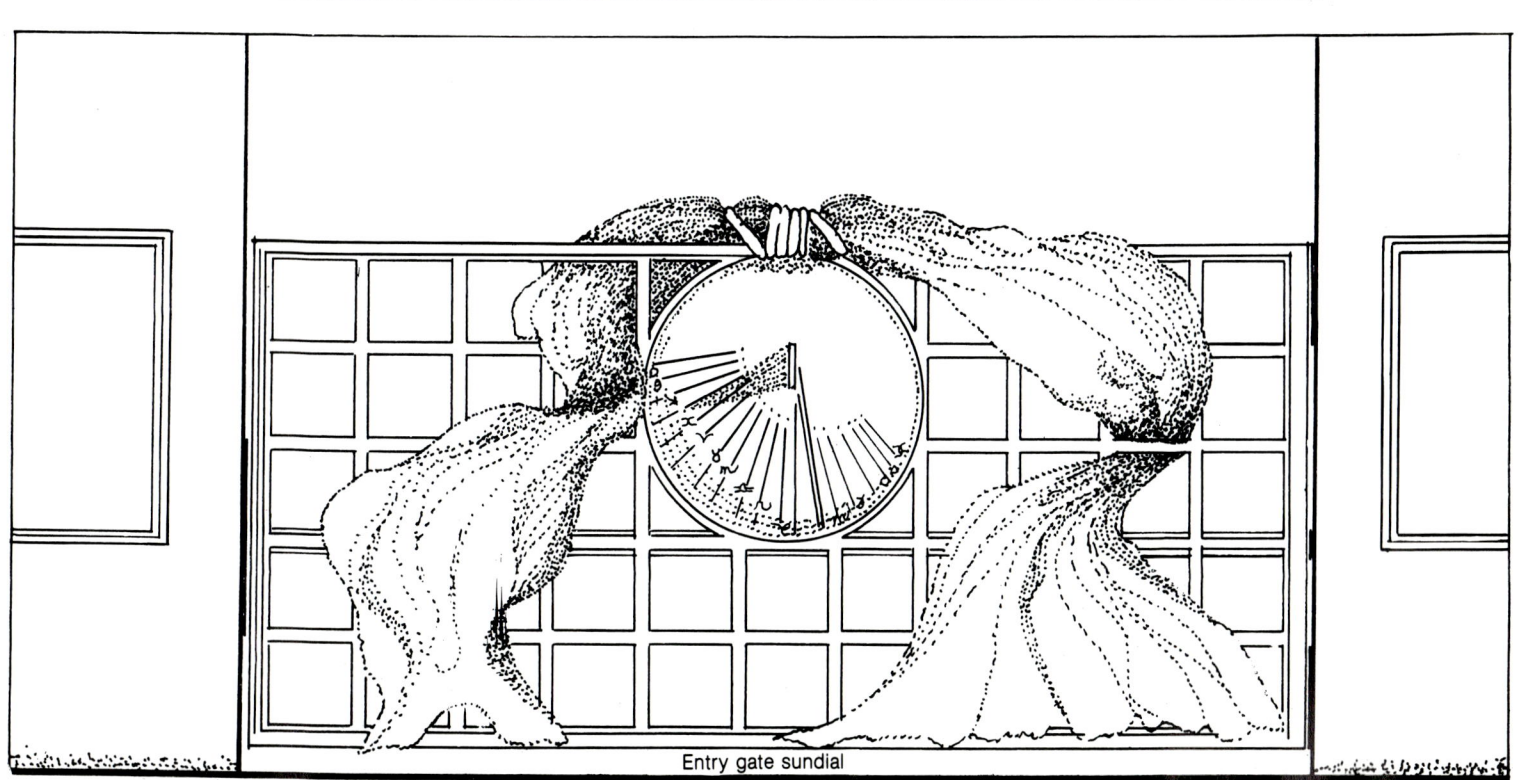
Entry gate sundial

Sexton Towers
Fort Smith, Arkansas, 1980, Latitude 35.22N

North entry

This is a HUD 202/8 highrise project for the elderly and disabled. The eight story 150 unit building is shaped by the positioning of the maximum number of dwelling units on the south and the servant elements of elevators and stairways to the north. The commons room takes on the form of a "Solar Module."

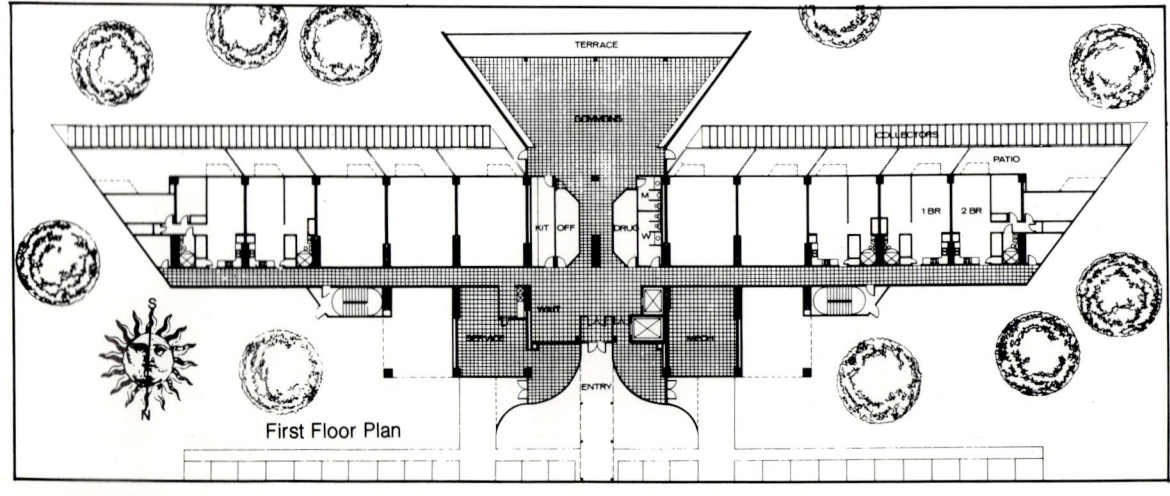

First Floor Plan

East Elevation

Berlin Housing Project
Berlin, Germany, 1981, Latitude 52.32N

"The low winter sun is captured in a "sunspace" that is an intermediate zone separating interior from exterior. The mass of the inner walls and floors act as the storage elements for the solar heat. The "sunspace" distributes solar heat directly to the apartments, control is by simple opening and closing of windows as the apartment requires for comfort. Plants will thrive in the sunspace where fruit trees and bushes will grow year round.

The scale and concept of the traditional housing neighborhood blocks are maintained in this design."

Jörg Ludwig, SOLAR 4, 1981

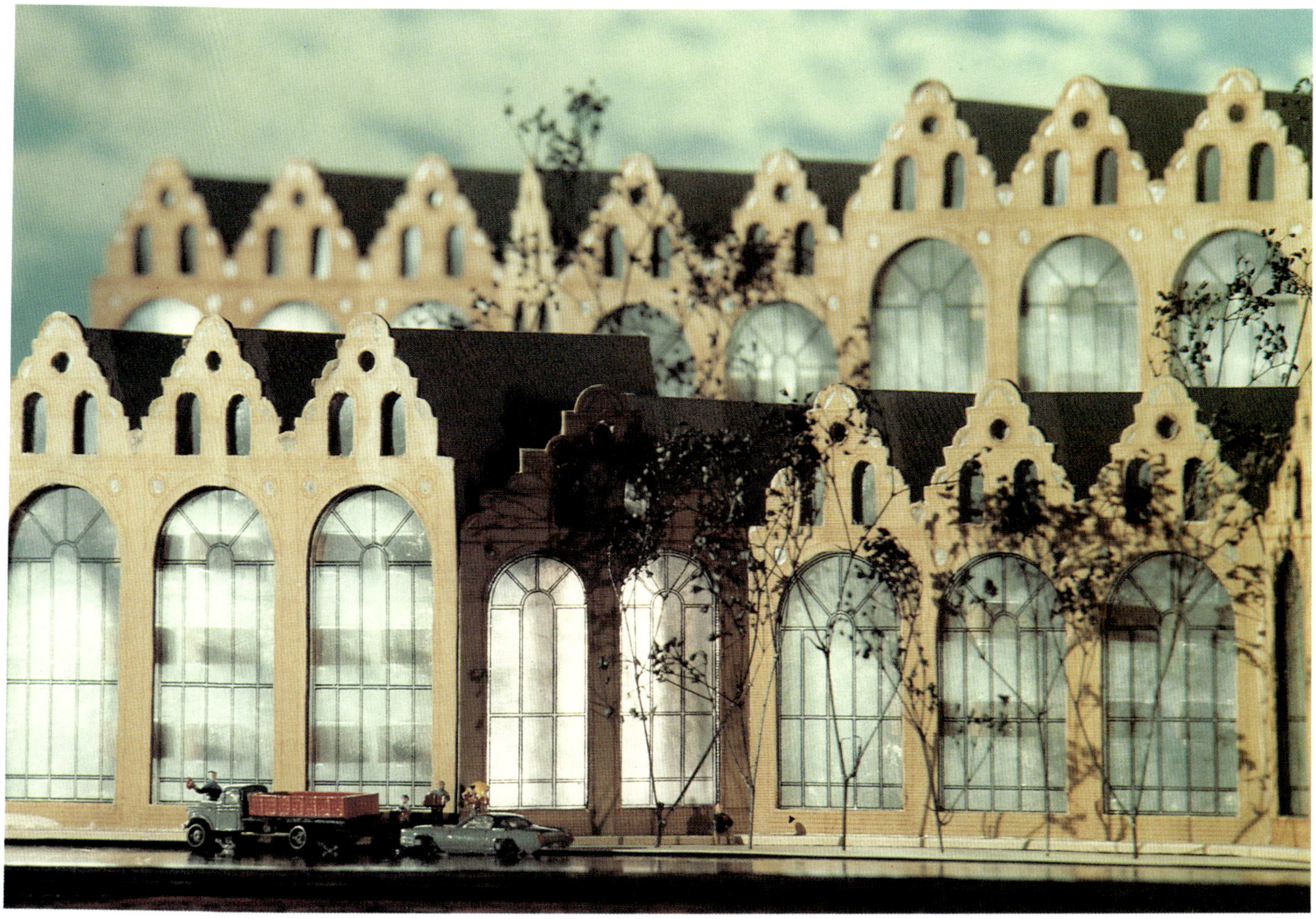

South Elevation with sunspace

Existing Site

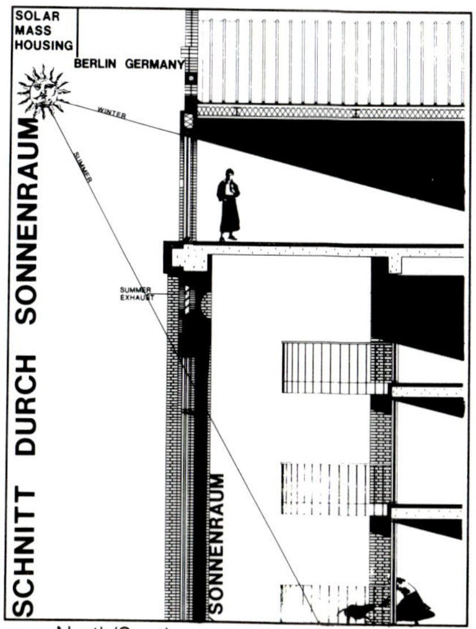

North/South section with sunspace

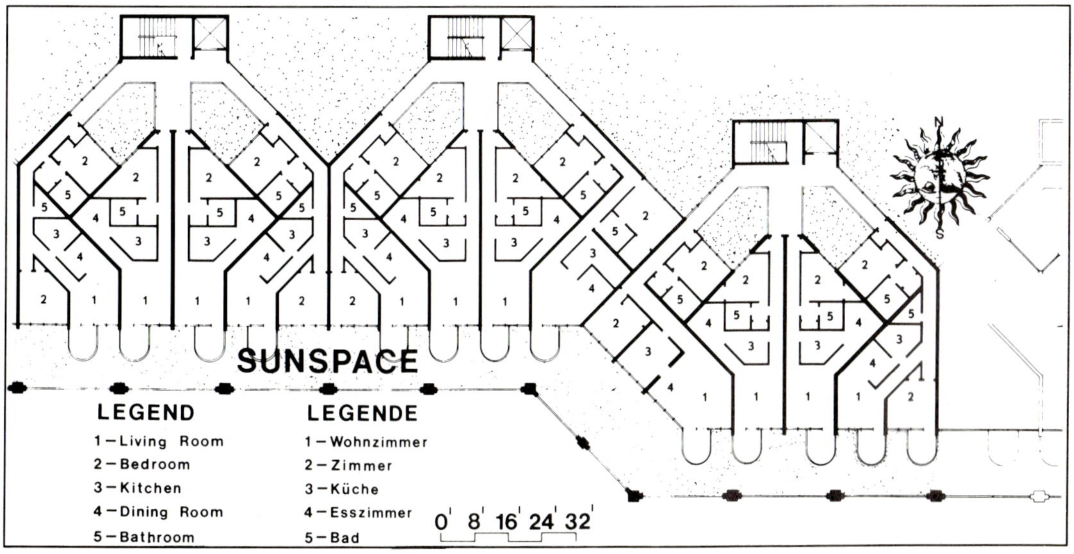

Floor Plan

SUNSPACE

LEGEND	LEGENDE
1 — Living Room	1 — Wohnzimmer
2 — Bedroom	2 — Zimmer
3 — Kitchen	3 — Küche
4 — Dining Room	4 — Esszimmer
5 — Bathroom	5 — Bad

SCHNITT DURCH SONNENRAUM

SOLAR MASS HOUSING
BERLIN GERMANY

Eagleridge Competition
Steamboat Springs, Colorado, 1981, Latitude 40.28N

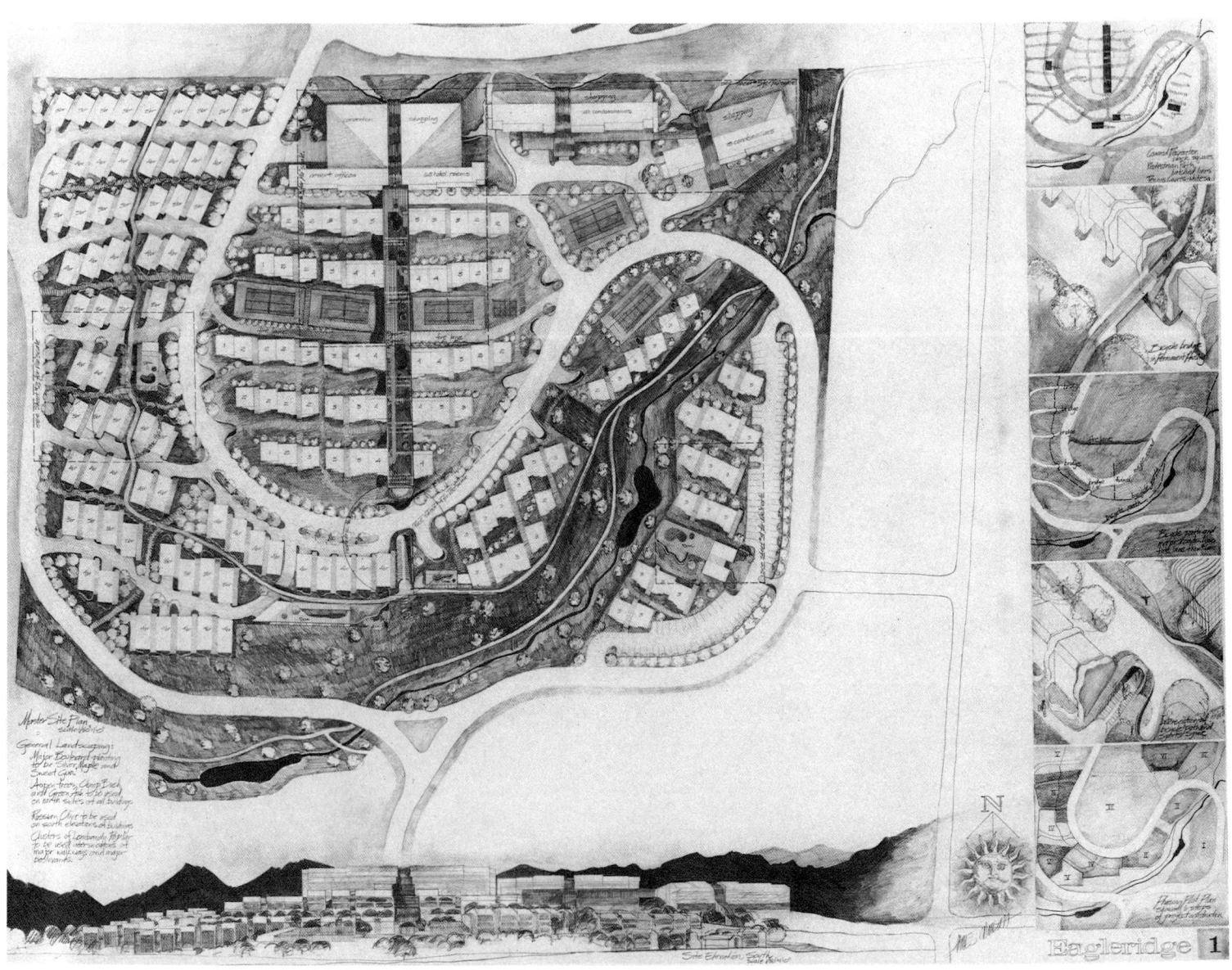

This design covers a 37 acre site. There are 341 condominiums, a 194 unit lodge and hotel, and 81,900 square feet of mixed use commercial, retail, and office space.

Lambeth's design is shaped along the site contours while giving every dwelling large amounts of south glass and views to the ski slopes beyond. Reflective glass ribbons wrap the entry axis becoming a snow melting reflective lens and then a sky light for the interior.

The recreation spine that cascades down the site from the hotel is also sheathed in reflective glass.

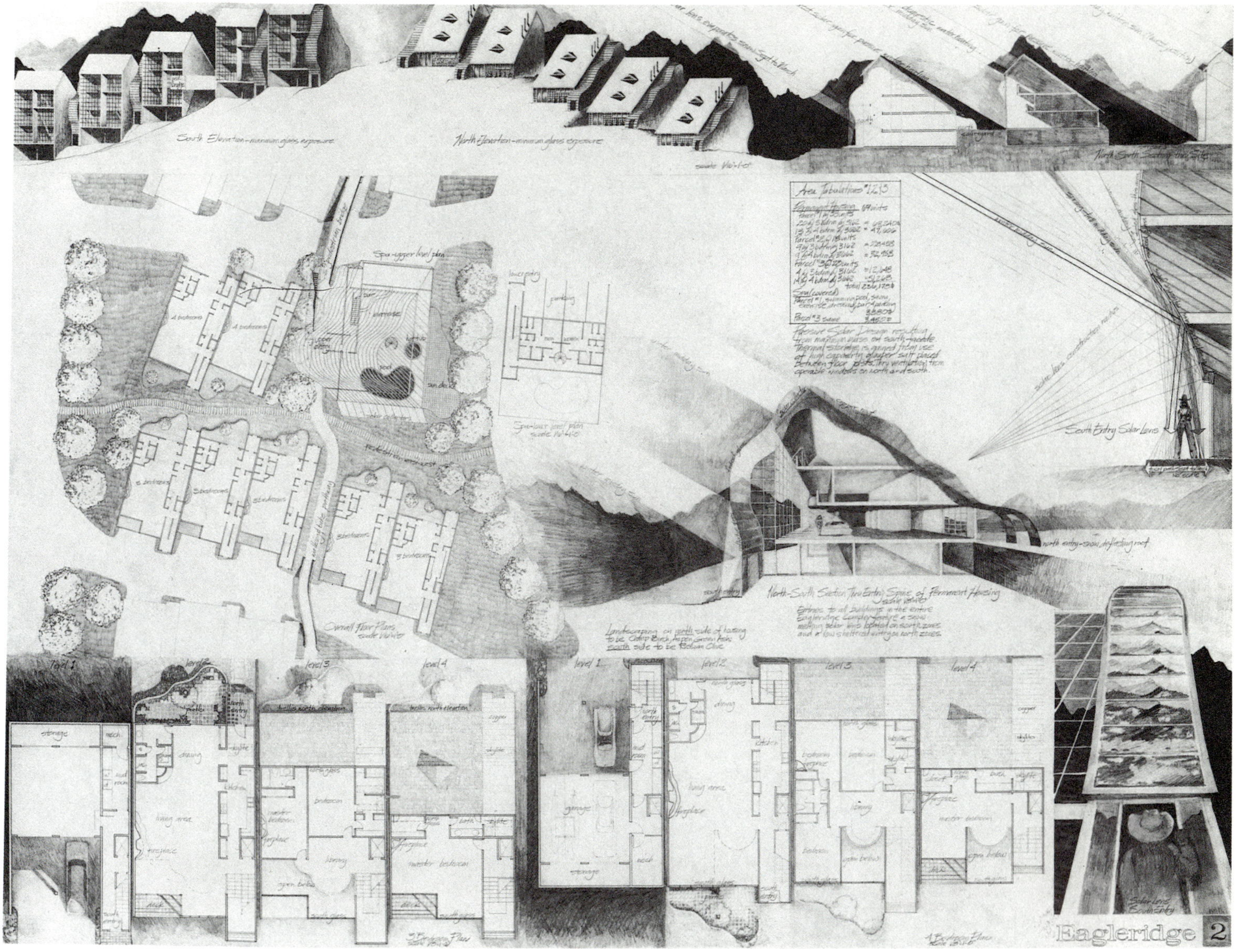

McAuley Residence
Ozark, Arkansas, 1981, Latitude 35.21N

The design of the McAuley residence paralleled the Eagleridge competition. The residence features a ribbon of reflective glass that protect the entry and allows light into the interior stairway.

North entry

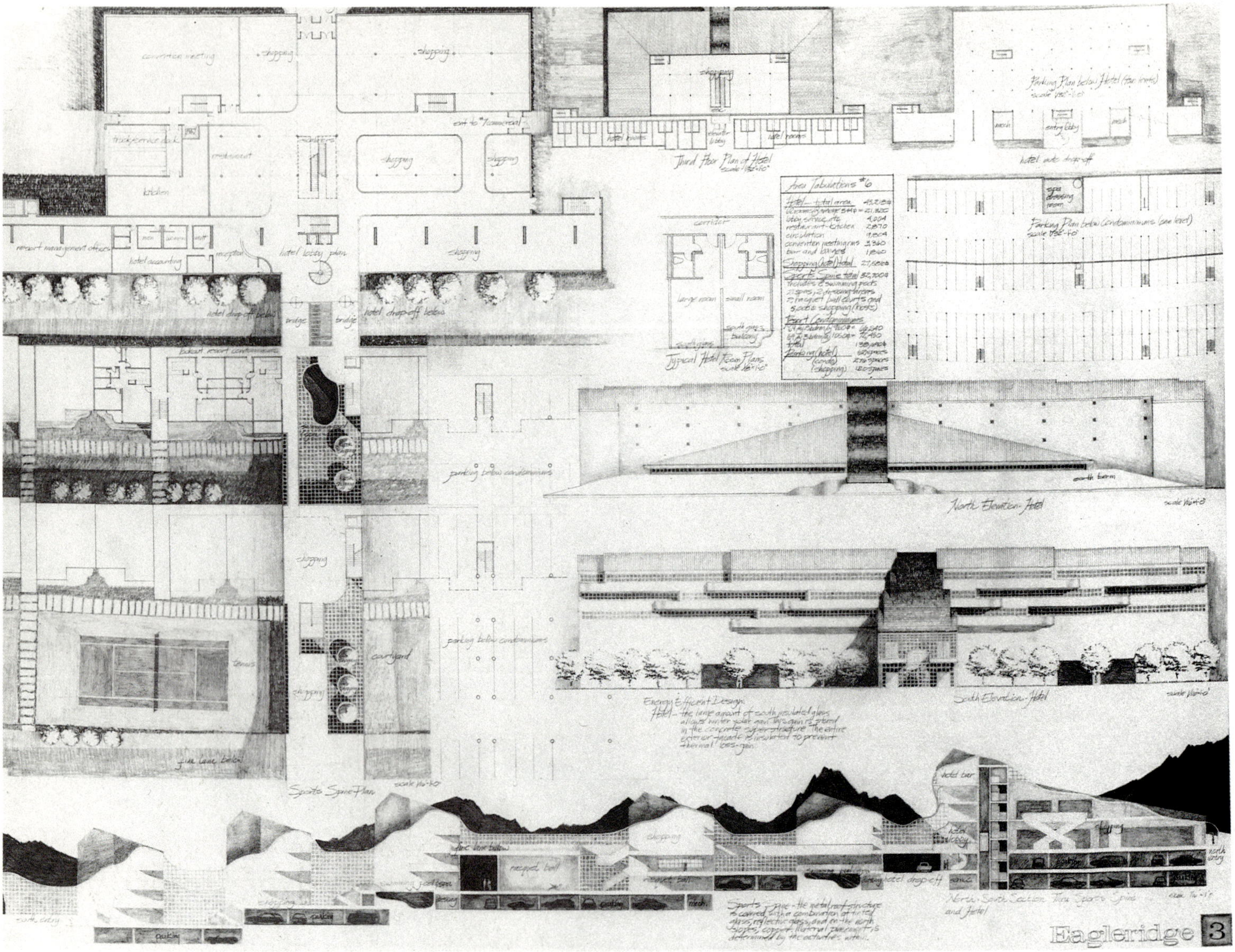

North Elevation

South Elevation

Tribune Tower Update
Chicago, Illinois, 1982, Latitude 41.50N

"Snow blowers are a big improvement over shoveling, no doubt about that, but there's still a certain element of misery involved; after all somebody has to be out there in all that cold pushing the machine. Well now, reports New Shelter magazine, there's a passive system that doesn't involve any effort on your part at all — at least for keeping the doorway clean and clear. James Lambeth has developed the no-work, solar snowplow. It works like this: Lambeth installed a 50-square-foot curved mirror above the south-facing doorway of a Colorado ski lodge. The gold-tinted mirror sweeps the sun's rays over a 200-square-foot path, raising the temperature to about 50 degrees Fahrenheit, which is warm enough to melt any snow on the sidewalk and steps. Lambeth was careful to tilt the device outward so that it blocked the high summer sun from reaching the mirror and parching the surrounding grass. We don't know how big a mirror you'd need to melt all the snow on your whole driveway in these climes, but we suspect that it might rival the Sears Tower and cause small forest fires besides."
Christine Winter, CHIGAGO TRIBUNE, 1982

Dear Ms. Winter:

Thank you for your mention in the Tribune last week. I have enclosed a design for a "snow melting solar lens" for your beautiful building. While clearing snow along Michigan Avenue, you should also see a marked increase in sunglasses being worn along the Magnificient Mile.

Sincerely, The uninvited late entrant to the "Tribune Tower Competition."

View of "Snow-melting Lens" from Michigan Ave.

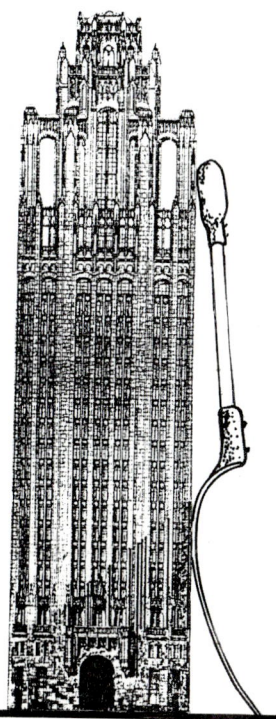
View of west entry and snow melting lens

Blevins High School
Blevins, Arkansas, 1982, Latitude 33.28N

Site from above

"The rolling site contains a scattering of buildings. Most of them were constructed in the thirties. The new facility must not only serve the existing junior high and gymnasium to the west but the elementary school to the east. The high school is designed as a corridor connecting these functions. The primary relationship with the elementary school is the new facilities' cafeteria and library. The gymnasium relates to the high school specialties to the west end of the structure"

Due to the extreme economic limitations of the agricultural community, a structure of modest cost and high energy efficiency was required. The building is composed of concrete block and standard agricultural steel frame and roof construction. Much of the work will be donated by the community, so the standard materials and simple design were essential.

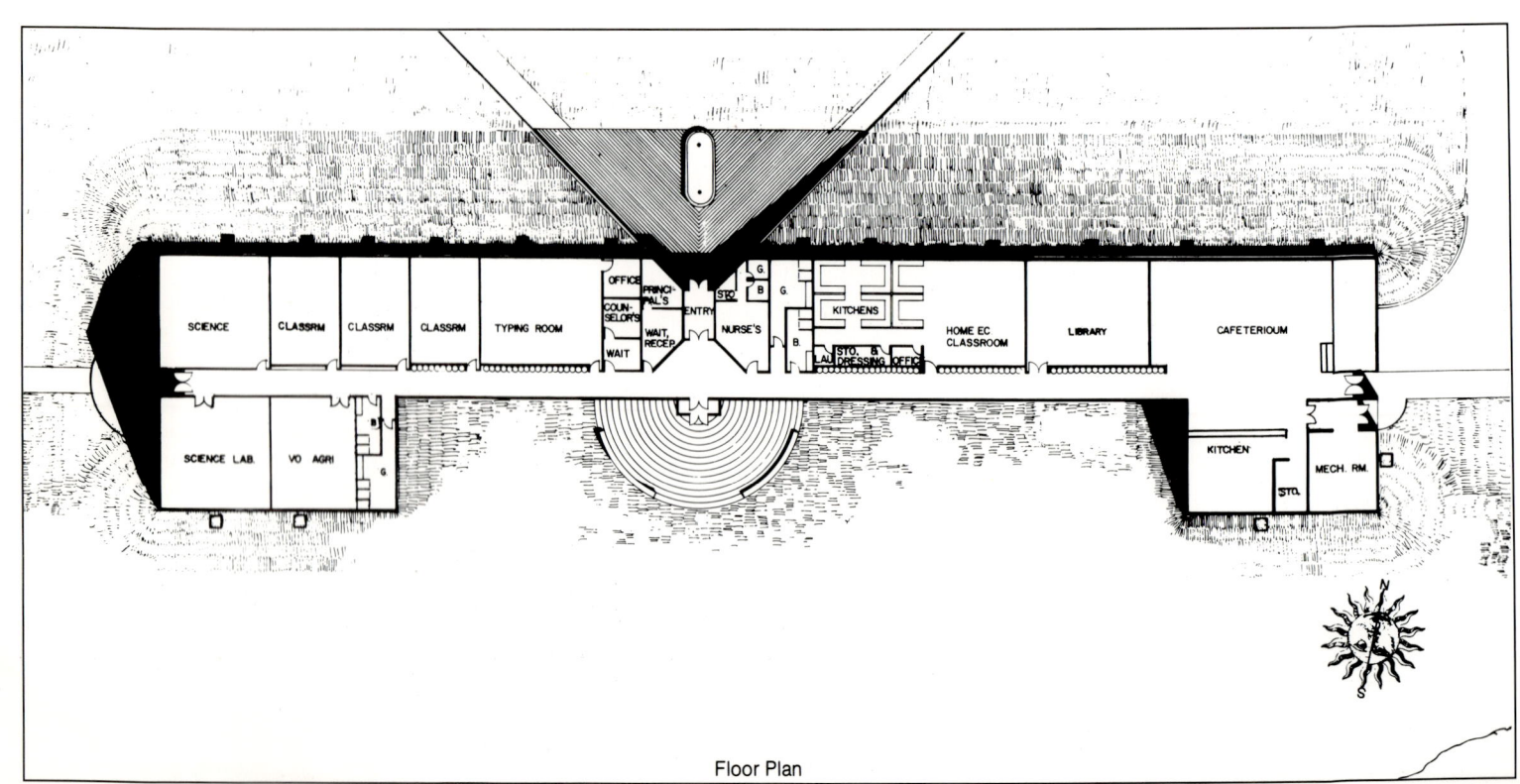

Floor Plan

View of main corridor

Energy efficiency was achieved by optimum orientation and good insulation. The north elevation is protected by an earth berm. High windows on this wall provide thru ventilation and natural daylighting to the classrooms. The south elevation is composed primarily of insulated glass. The passive solar design of the facility is based on the penetration of the low winter sun into the south corridor. The solar energy is stored in the mass of the concrete floor and the water of the 55 gallon drums of water. The stored energy is slowly released and passes through openings in the classroom wall. Individual air handlers located in the attic provide for added circulation and back-up heat when necessary. The south corridor is totally shaded in the summer.

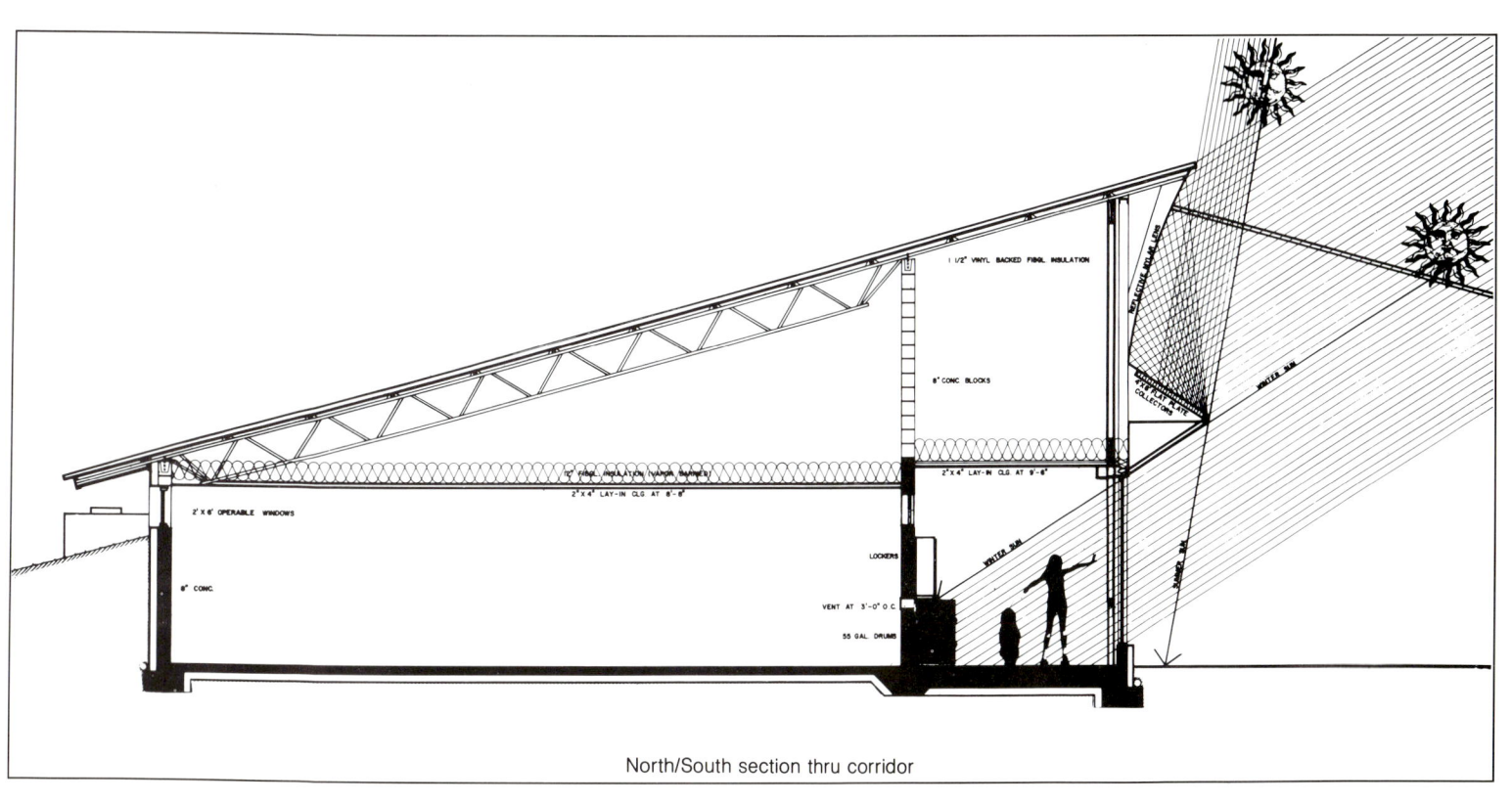
North/South section thru corridor

Detail of solar lens

The hot water demands of the building are large. The cafeteria not only feeds all the school students, but also supplies hot lunches to the senior citizens of the area. All of the energy to heat the water will be provided by the school made solar collectors and solar reflector of the south elevation. The reflector doubles the energy collected by the system. The prismatic aluminum mylar surface of the lens will also reflect a constantly changing rainbow pattern to the students and community during the day. Summer canning facilities will also be provided by the new building. This new structure will provide the community with a pride and focus for activities. It will also give a direction for the new schools of Arkansas.''
L'ARCHITECTURE D'AUJOURD'HUI, 1980

South elevation at midafternoon

South elevation at late afternoon

Peak International Competition
Victoria Peak, Hong Kong, 1982, Latitude 22.29N

View of northwest

The design of this project is based on an attempt to harmonize with the site and take full advantage of its spectacular location, while adhering to the principles of Feng-Shui to ensure prosperity for the occupants. The building is envisioned as an abstract continuation of the mountain itself. As it rises from the ground it takes on the crystalline aspect of a geological formation being pushed upward by the forces of the earth. By conceiving the building as an extension of its site, the mountain is allowed to maintain its dignity and does not simply become a backdrop for an architectural monument. As the modular living units rise to the upper levels a large protected space is formed beneath them which becomes the public areas in the center section and a private swimming area in the northern section. The stepped geometries of the living units allows each one to have at least one outdoor deck on the roof of the unit below. Some units have as much private outdoor space as inside space, and every unit has a vast view to the city and bay below.

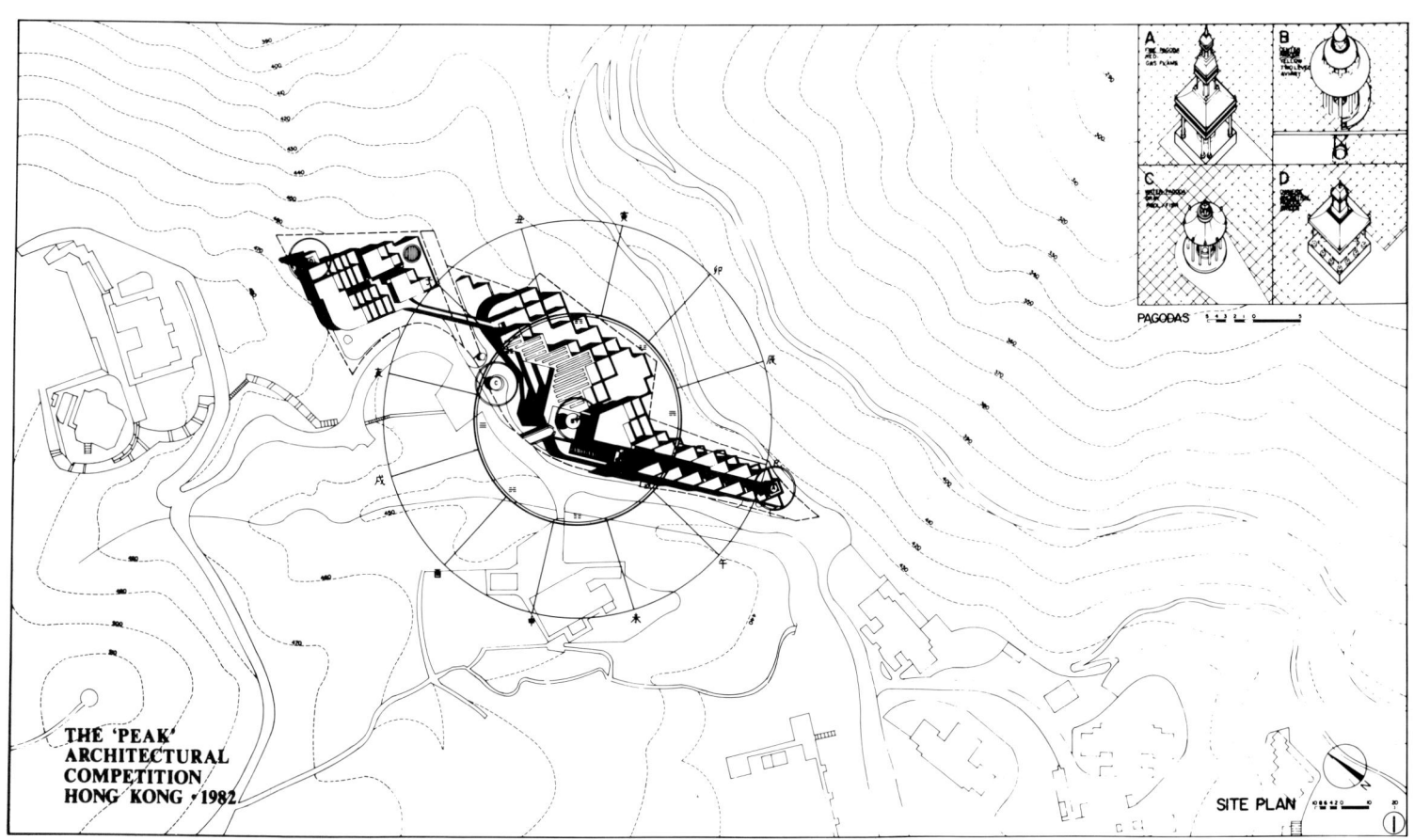

THE 'PEAK'
ARCHITECTURAL
COMPETITION
HONG KONG 1982

SITE PLAN

The principles of Feng-Shui are followed throughout the design. The main entry is parallel to the line of the green dragon and is at an angle to the main road, and all entries to living units are at an angle to the main circulation paths to block evil spirits from entering. Pagodas are placed at each of the geomantic positions and are colored according to Feng-Shui principles; yellow for the center position, red for the fire position and gray for the water position, another pagoda is provided for the private use of the promotors family to bring extra good fortune and is green since it is on the east side. Entrances to the site are protected by pagodas and pagodas mark the northern and southern limits of the site.

The west side is shaded and has soft curves to express the "yin", while the east side is bright and powerful which expresses the "yang". Effort is made to bring the essential elements into balance. Pools are kept small to avoid an excess of water influences which are abundant because of the nearness of the bay, and shutters and floors of teakwood provide the wood influence. Concrete and steel reinforcing provide the elements of earth and metal, while solar collectors absorb the fire of the sun.

Comfort and solar control are achieved mainly through the use of materials and cross-ventilation. All windows are operable and have teak shutters for sun control. Exterior walls are of glazed clay tiles which reflect the sun and are vented to exhaust day heat, the interior is wrapped with insulation. Solar collectors on the roof of the middle section provide hot water and supplement the heating system. In bright sunlight the building appears pure white, a glistening gem set into the mountain, but as the sun gets lower in the sky, a subtle gradation of color is revealed — pale green at the base turning to a faint blue at the top reflecting the forest below and the sky above and providing an elegant link between earth and sky.

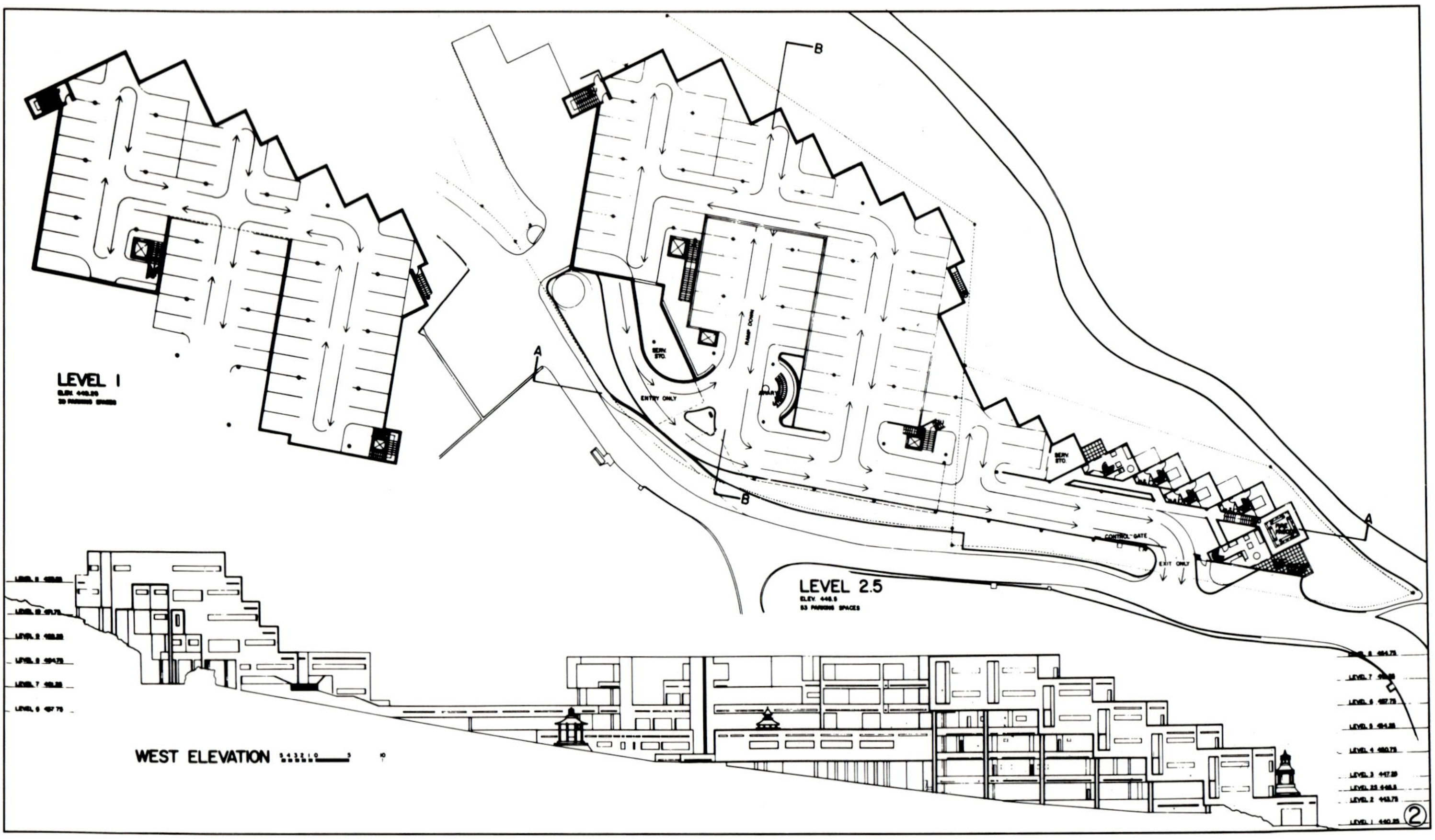

LEVEL 1

WEST ELEVATION

LEVEL 2.5

View looking east with Hong Kong

View looking west

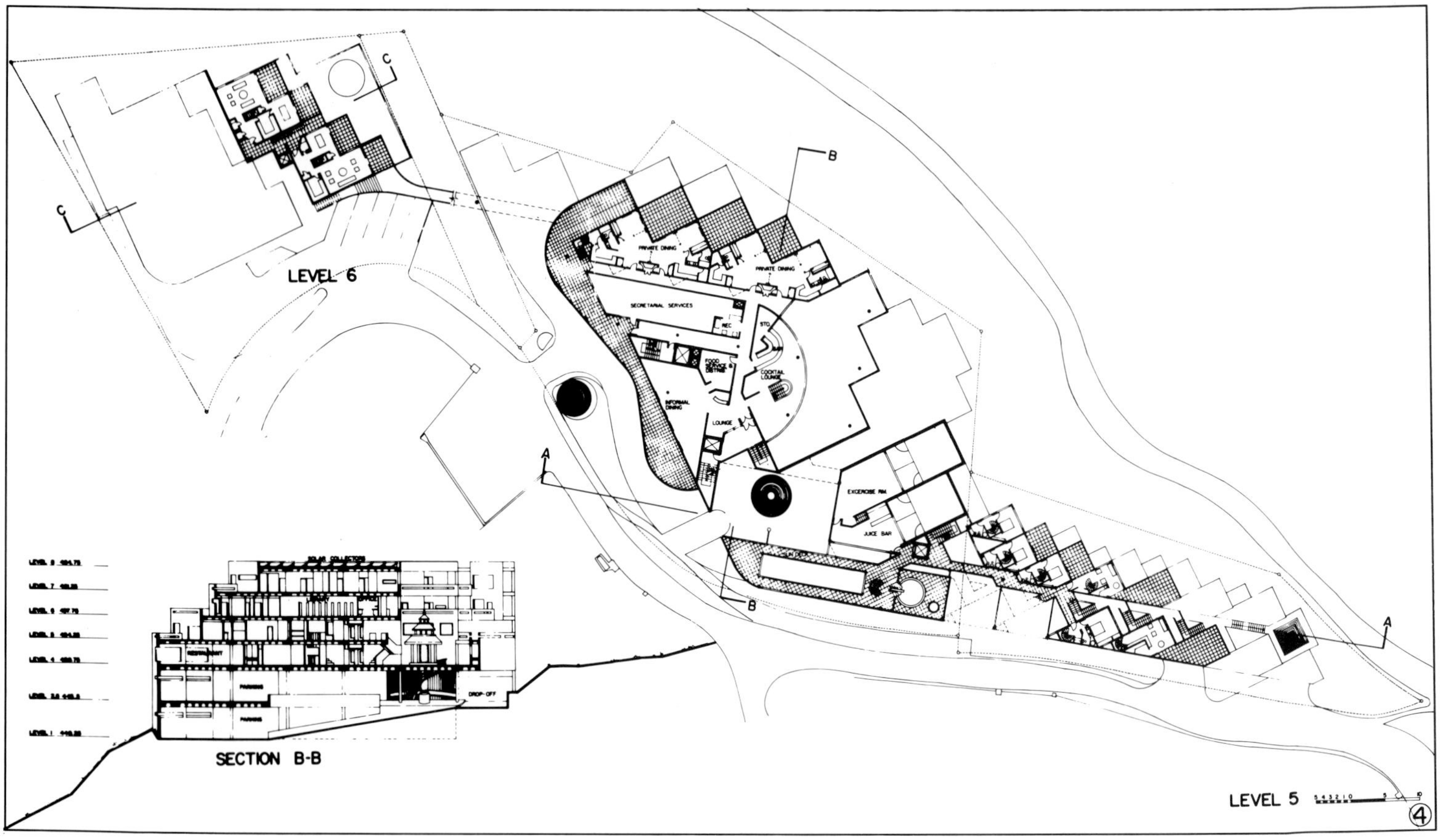

Pagoda at entry with aviary

Owner's pagoda and pool

Juice bar with squash court

Major dining room

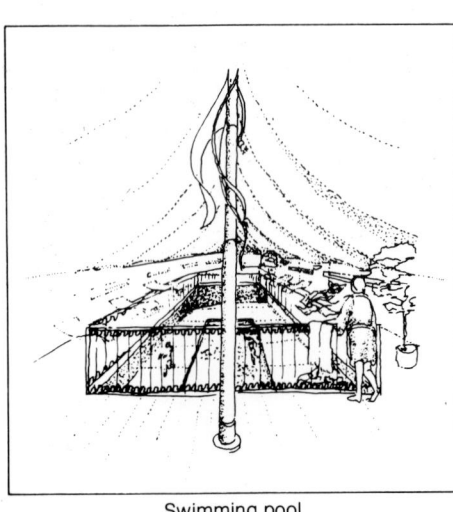
Swimming pool

Owner's living room

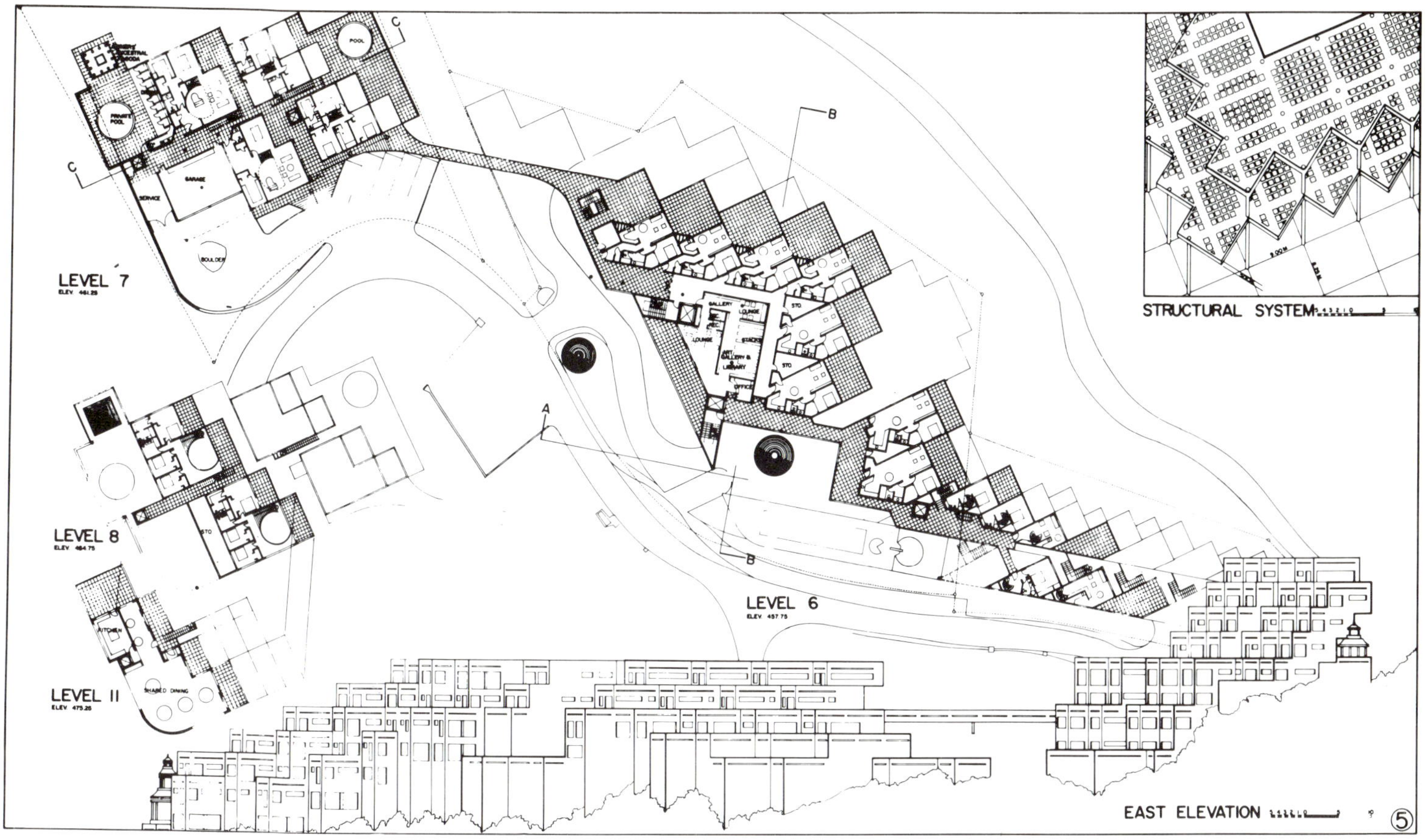

View looking north

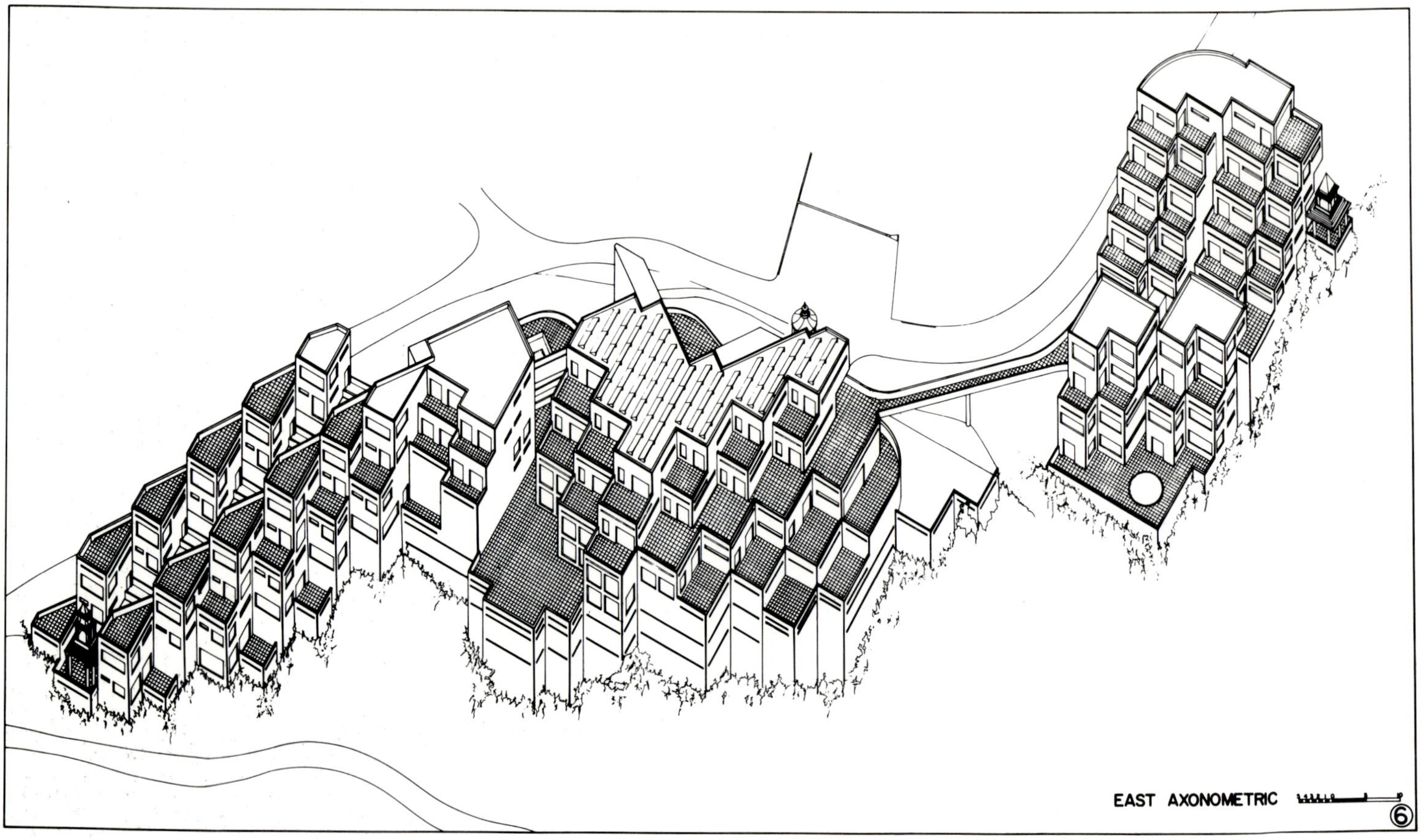

EAST AXONOMETRIC ⑥

View of southeast

Sculpture Gallery
Santa Fe, New Mexico, 1982, Latitude 36.34N

This is a study in optimum solar form. The main gallery space is full of sun from sunrise to sunset in the winter months. During summer months the interior is totally shaded.

There is a mezzanine level exhibition space and below ground is located service facilities and a small area to display drawings and paintings.

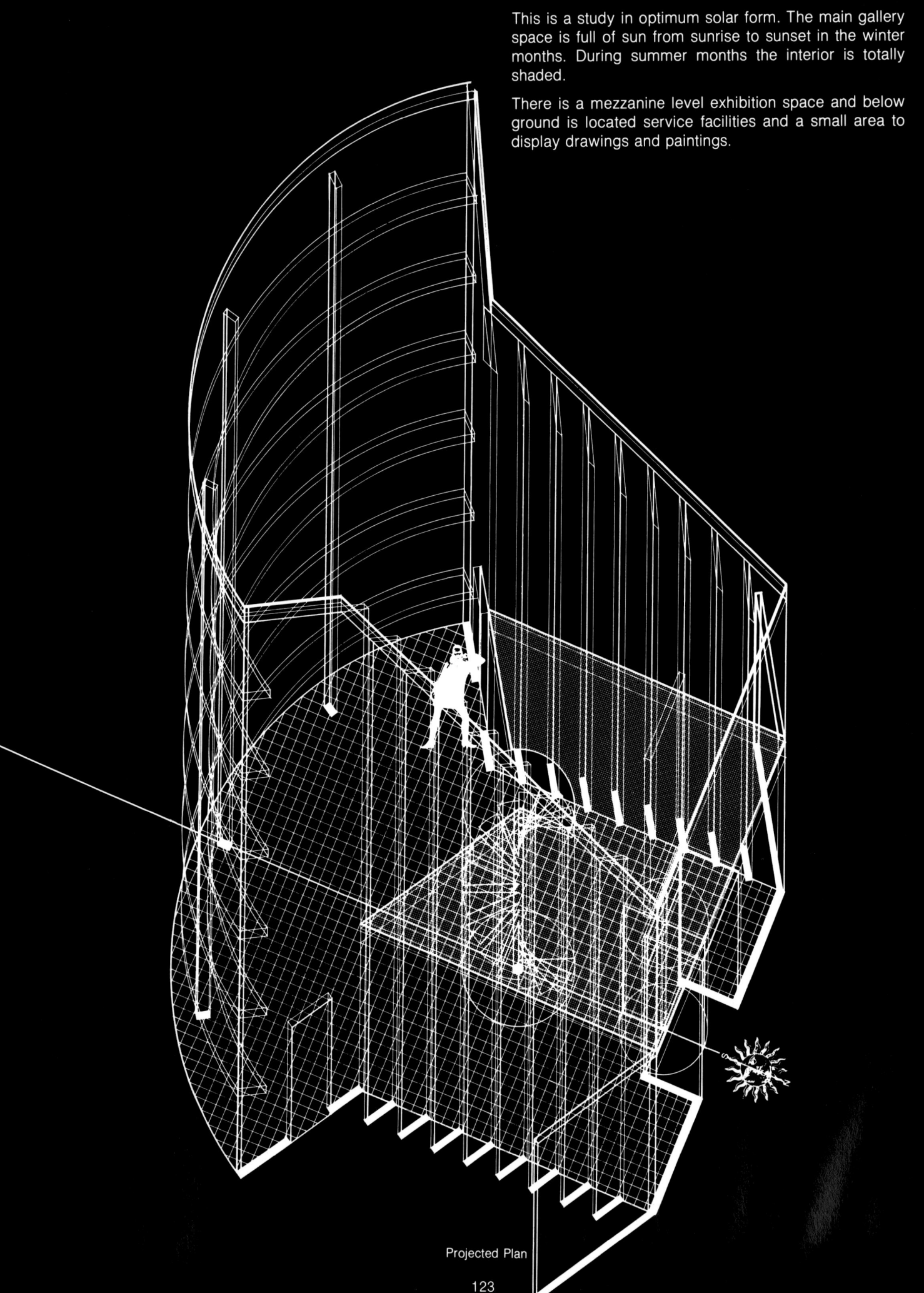

Projected Plan

Desert Compound
Amargosa Desert, Nevada, 1983, Latitude 36.17N

View of south walls

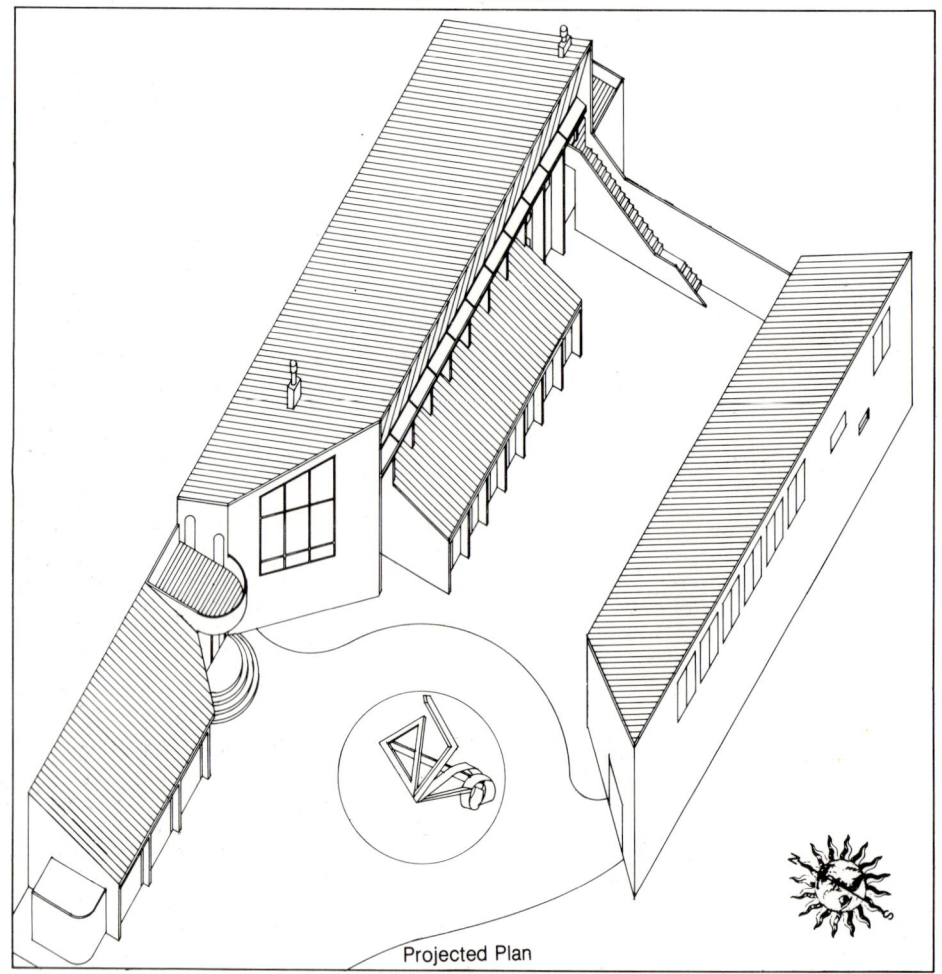

Projected Plan

Opposite: View of northeast elevation

This compound is formed around a courtyard. The north structure contains a swimming pool and gymnasium on the first level and a two bedroom residence on the second level. The southern structure is an art studio.

The desert climate limited the amount of glass. The mirror glass of the large angled clerestory reflects energy onto a bank of solar collectors. The heated water is for domestic use and for the swimming pool.

Entry sculpture

View of site looking east

Detail of east wall

View of collectors and reflective windows

Southeast Elevation

Opposite: Detail of east wall

Gary Lambeth Residence
Springfield, Missouri, 1984, Latitude 37.11N

Column studies

The main design determinant in this design is the client's exotic car collection. As in an early Mies van der Rohe design, the favorite car of the day is parked in the glass inset in the living room. The courtyard features a swimming pool that meets the master bedroom. The water reflects low winter sun into the south facing rooms. Guest quarters are located in the three story entry tower.

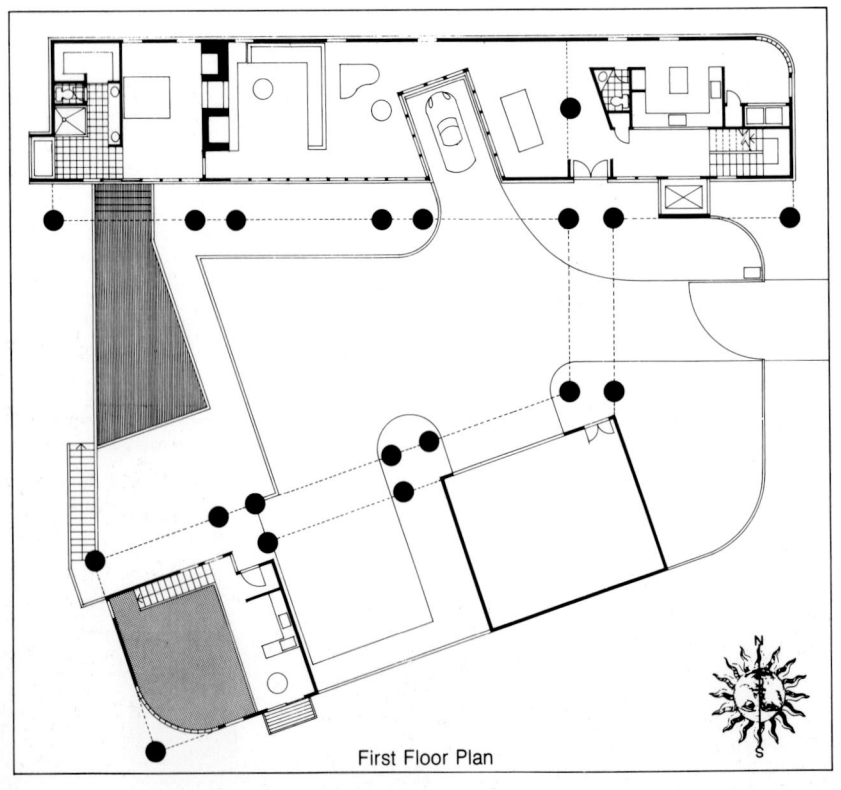

First Floor Plan

View of entry looking west

Sundial study for exterior glazed tile mural

Best Inns Motel
Springfield, Missouri, 1985, Latitude 37.11N

Above and Below: View of Solar Lens and pool

Best Inns Motel
Joplin, Missouri, 1986, Latitude 37.04N

Above: Entry from the east

Below: Solar Lens Detail

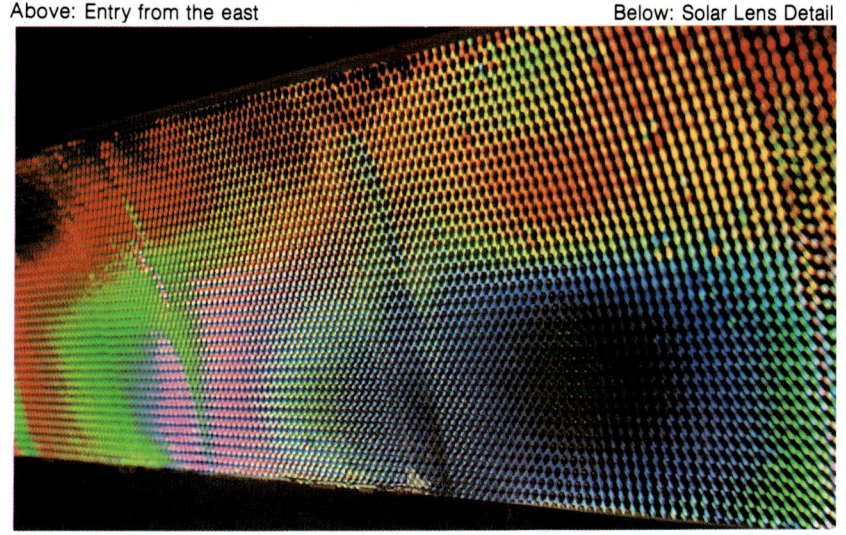

Sphinx Paintings
Cairo, Egypt, 1987, Latitude 30.03N

135

Hedges Residence and Guest House
Springfield, Missouri, 1988, Latitude 37.11N

Evening view of south elevation

The residence is approached from the north on a winding drive through a densely wooded area. Upon arrival to the residence, the north face is seen with few windows. The drive-thru frames a panoramic view of a meadow to the south. The south elevation is almost totally glass. A massive 4'x4' gridded aluminum wisteria trellis protects the decks and interior in the summer while allowing penetration of the sun in the winter. Exterior surface material is dryvit, limestone and granite. The roof is standing ribbed metal. The living room is designed for large parties and opens above to the master bedroom and bridged library. The three-level tower to the east contains a garage on the first level, auxiliary bedroom on the second, and a computer room on the top. The lowest level has a den and opens to a dog-run below the house. Interior materials are marble and bleached oak floors. Walls are painted plaster. The architect also designed the main entry door, chairs, tables, lighting fixtures, and paintings for the home. The compound also has a guest house located to the south of the main house.

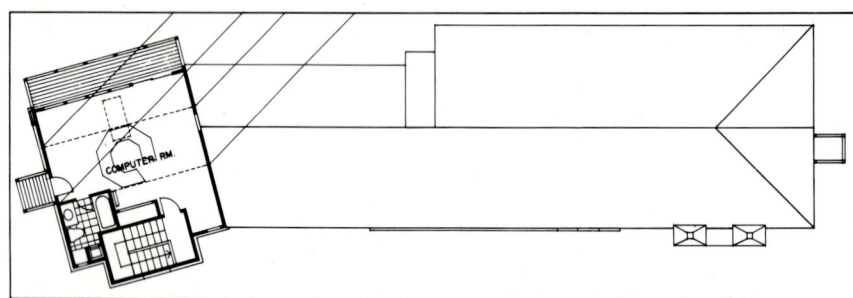

Third Floor Plan

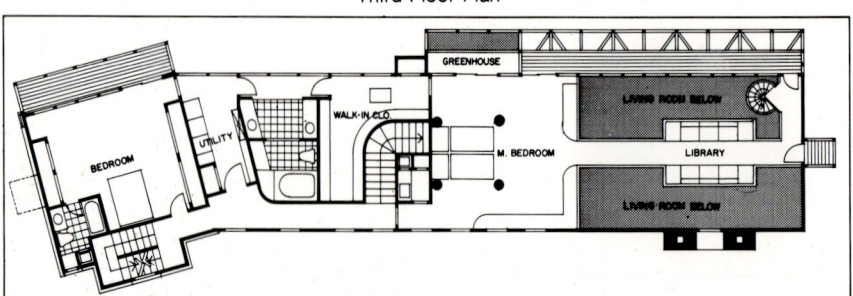

Second Floor Plan

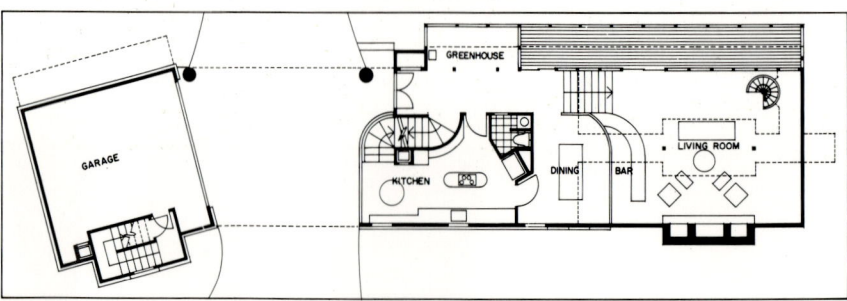

First Floor Plan

Aerial view of the site from the south

Above and below: View of north entry and drive-thru　　　　Opposite: Front door with site abstraction with onyx

View of master bedroom and bridge library

View of living room

Above: View looking east   Opposite: Settee of natural birch, leather, and marble

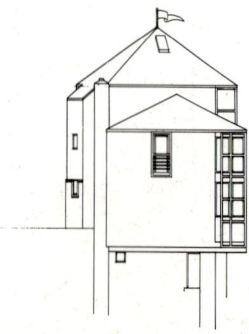

The Hedges' guest house is located 300 yards to the south of the main residence. It is a literal fragment of the main house's drive-thru. The entry curved glass block wall, lavender concrete column and entry plane are yen-yang duplicates of the main house.

The guest house steps into Pearson creek. A curved entry ramp wraps around a large oak tree and floats above the water. The solar efficiency of the fan shaped design is gained through large amounts of south glass allowing low winter sun and massive overhang shading the interior in the summer. Exterior materials are dryvit, limestone and granite. Interior materials are bleached oak and marble floors and painted plaster walls. The protective north wall has only one window, a fireplace and bath. A recessed circular tub/shower is located as part of the living area. Water controls are located in the lavender column. Privacy is maintained by a sliding circular curtain. A second level is a sleeping loft.

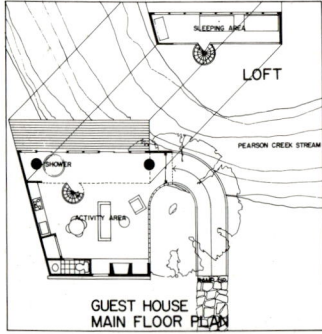

GUEST HOUSE MAIN FLOOR PLAN

Above: South Elevation

Opposite: East Elevation

Piney Grove Methodist Church
Hot Springs, Arkansas, 1988, Latitude 34.30N

North elevation showing main entry

South Elevation

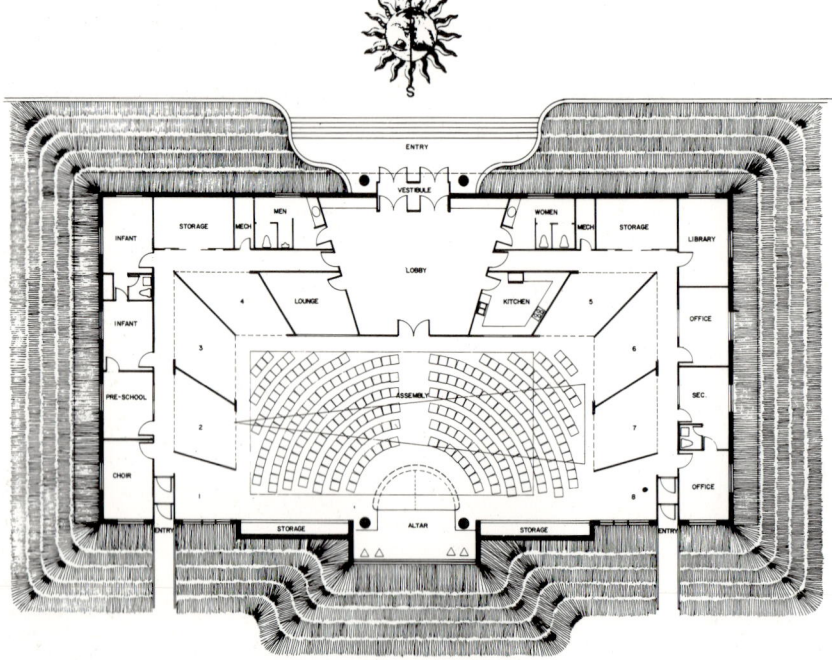

This church has earth bermed walls on the north, east, and west. The south is full glass.

The internal church auditorium is structured by walls that radiate from the altar. Classrooms are formed between the walls for smaller group meetings.

Large liquid-filled prisms are positioned behind the altar to create rainbows across the auditorium during morning services.

Watercolor of form composition

Miller Residence
Pittsburg, Kansas, 1989, Latitude 37.25N

This residence was designed for a photographer/composer.

A three level curved stairway is located at the intersection of two linear forms. The studio of the second level takes on the form of a grand piano.

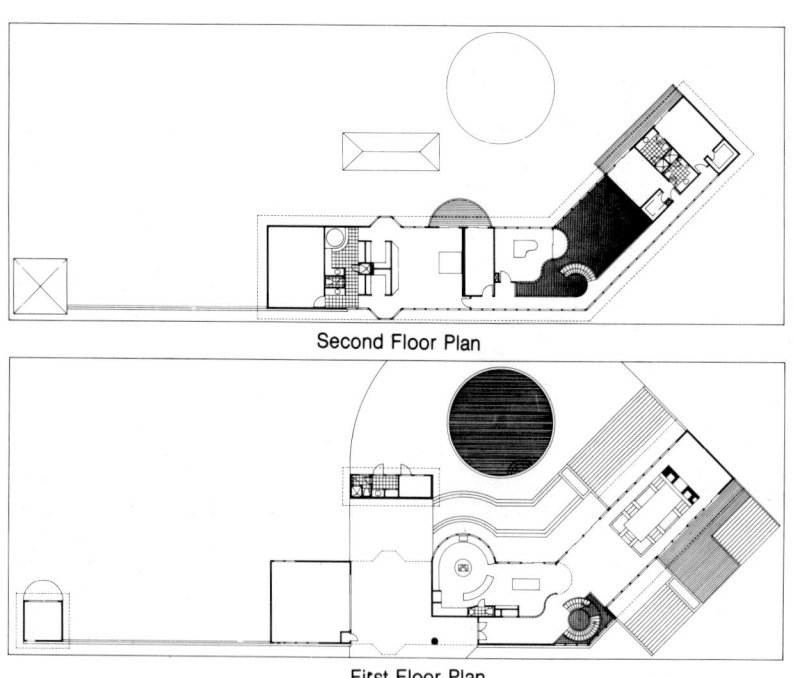

Second Floor Plan

First Floor Plan

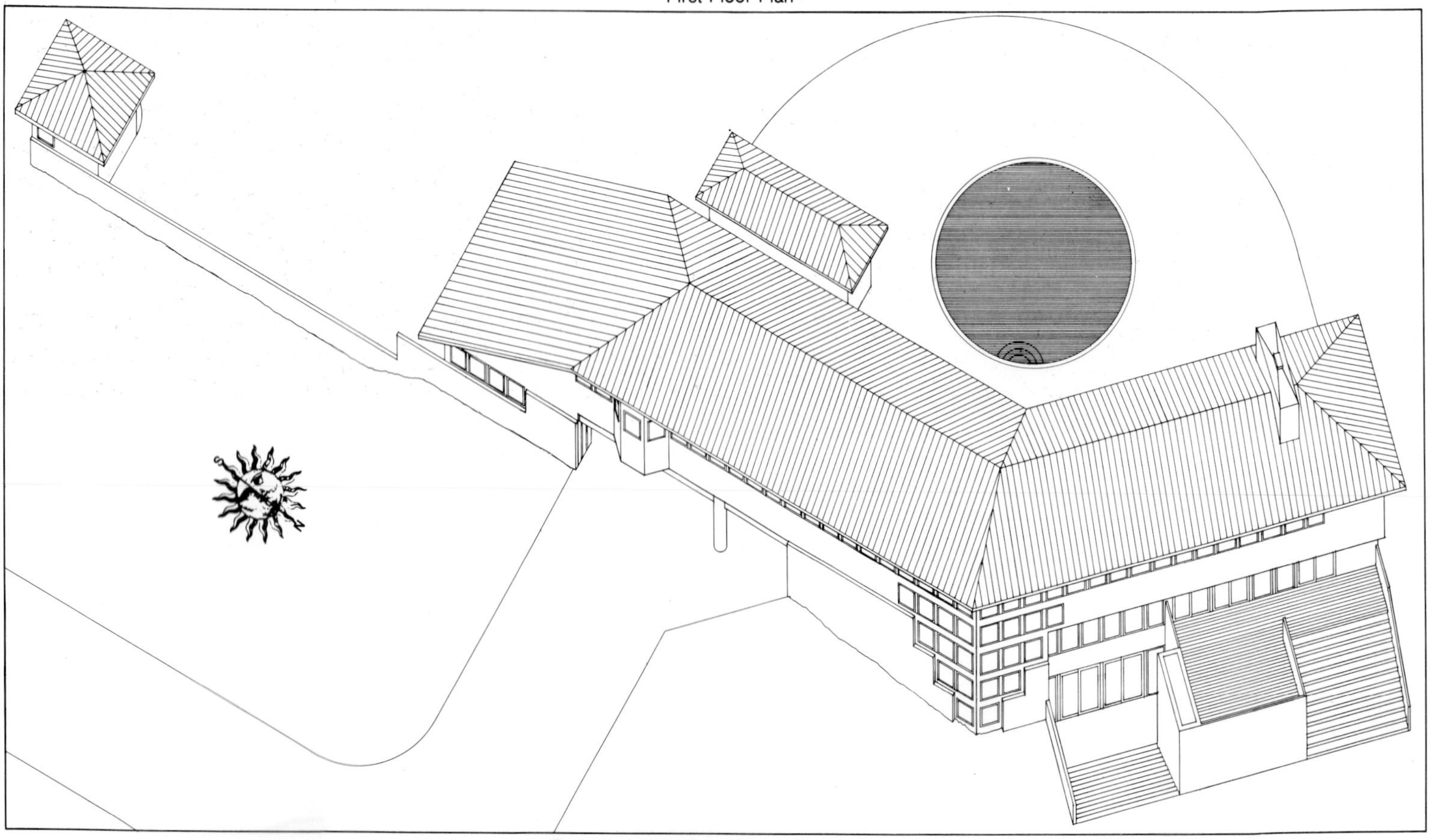

Projected plan of northeast elevation

Northeast elevation

View of living room and photographs

View of living room toward dining room and studio

View of stairway looking up

Davenport Residence
New Smyrna Beach, Florida, 1990, Latitude 29.01N

View from the waterway

View of north elevation from waterway

High ceilings, large overhangs, and maximum thru ventilation create a cool interior for this Florida residence located on the Intracoastal Waterway.

View of entry and north elevation

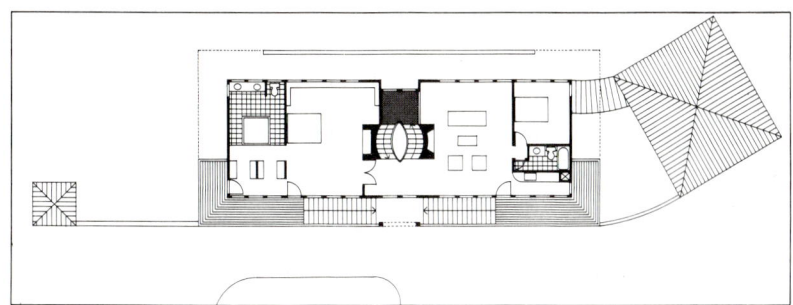

Second Floor Plan

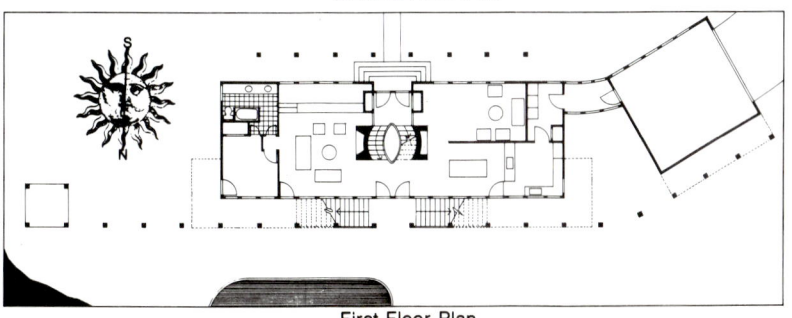

First Floor Plan

Leslie Residence
Harrison, Arkansas, 1991, Latitude 36.13N

The residence is located in a forrest in north central Arkansas. The basic rules of passive solar design are integrated into this design. The north is protected by massive walls covered in stucco and polished marble. The south is open to the winter sun with the pool reflecting additional solar radiation into the interior of the structure. Thermal storage is provided by marble surfaces covering concrete substructure. The glass entry is etched with a special sundial and is marked above with a translucent panel of onyx.

North entry

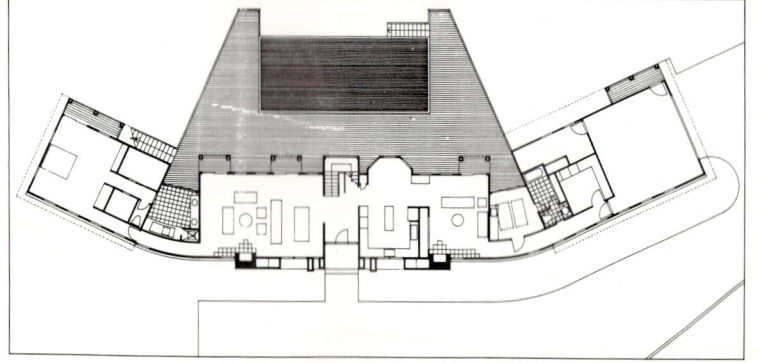

First Floor Plan

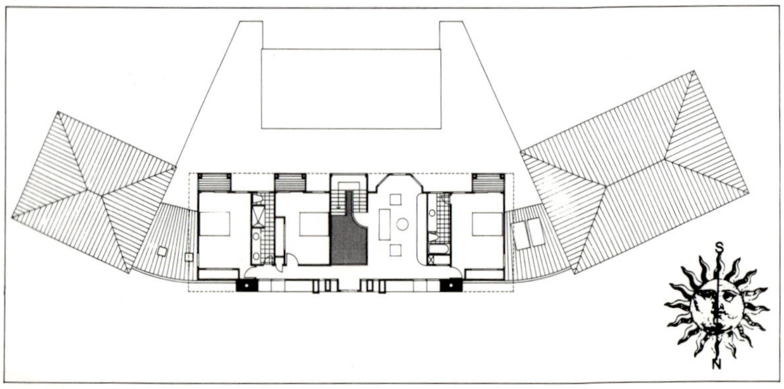

Second Floor Plan

Detail of entry door and sun-dial

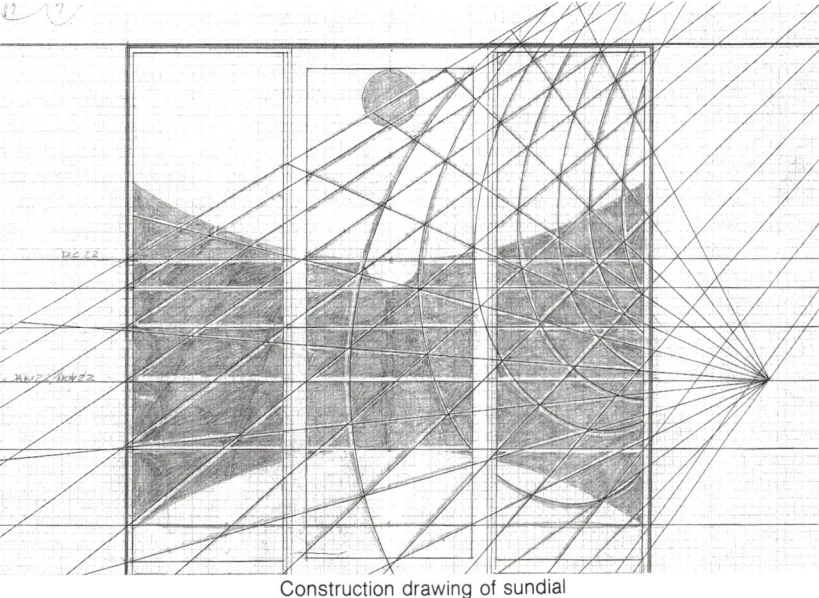
Construction drawing of sundial

Opposite: Entry settee with leather and onyx   Above: Entry looking down

View of living room looking north

View of den looking north

South Elevation and Swimming Pool

Yeager Residence
Estes Park, Colorado, 1992, Latitude 40.24N

This residence is designed as a stairway, stepping down the site through three levels, and culminating on an exterior deck. The procession constantly unfolds an increasingly magnificent view of the Rocky Mountains to the south.

Above: View of south elevation   Opposite: Twilight view of west elevation

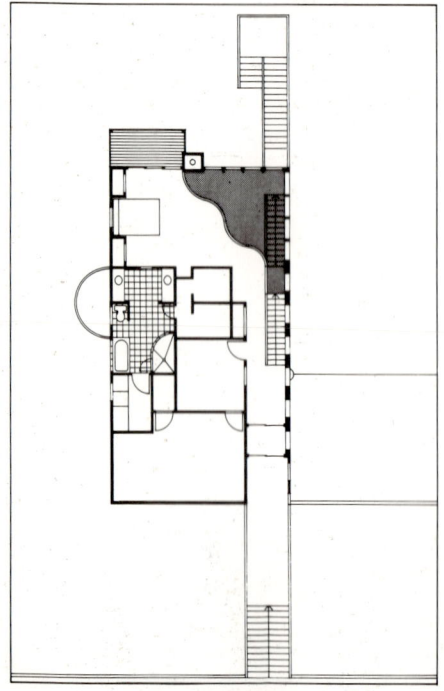

Third Floor Plan

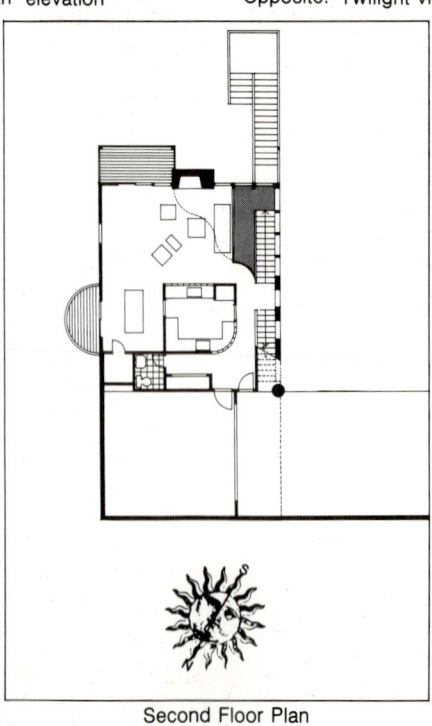

Second Floor Plan

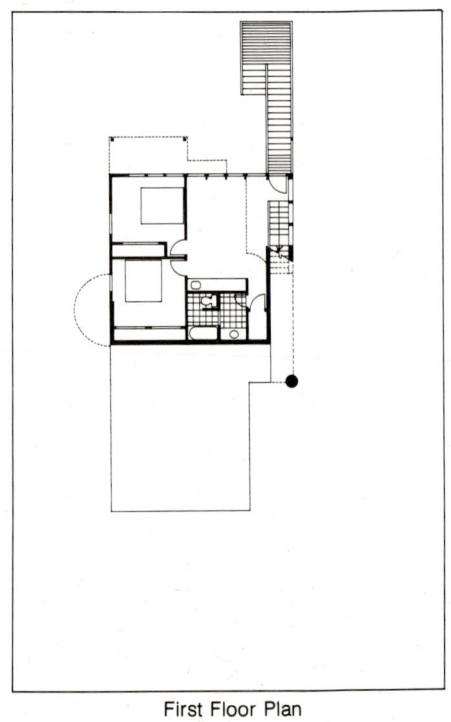

First Floor Plan

Opposite: View of South elevation   Above: West Elevation   Below: View of entry and north elevation

Above: Master bedroom looking down   Opposite: View of living room looking south

Above: Master Bathroom					Opposite: Master bedroom looking down

Entry bench with leather and marble

Opposite: View of Southeast Elevation

Inn at the Mill
Johnson, Arkansas, 1992, Latitude 36.08N

Pre-Civil War photo showing 40' wheel

This small historic Inn is the first project that James Lambeth has designed utilizing an existing structure listed on the National Historic Register.

First legally registered as a tax-paying business in 1835, the mill has the distinction of being the longest running business in the state of Arkansas, and possibly the longest continually operated mill in the nation.

Following the Civil War battle of Pea Ridge, Arkansas, in 1862, the mill was partially burned down by retreating Confederate renegades to prevent it from falling into the hands of the Federal forces. The Battle of Pea Ridge holds the notoriety of being the only battle in which Cherokees joined the Confederate troops against Union forces. The mill was reconstructed in 1867.

The architect decided to restore the historic structure and add a new wing of thirty rooms to the east. The new wing bridges across the auto entry and connects to the historic structure on the second level.

The interior of the mill was opened to create a three-level lobby. The top-level suites have internal balconies which view the entire three-story space through a structural grid of black walnut posts and beams.

Green marble marks the traditional building while a checker-board pattern of carrara and travertine marble designates the new structure.

The design is phased to have an additional twenty rooms extending to the east and north.

Above: Retreating Confederates burning mill 1862

Opposite: Mill 1992

View of south elevation

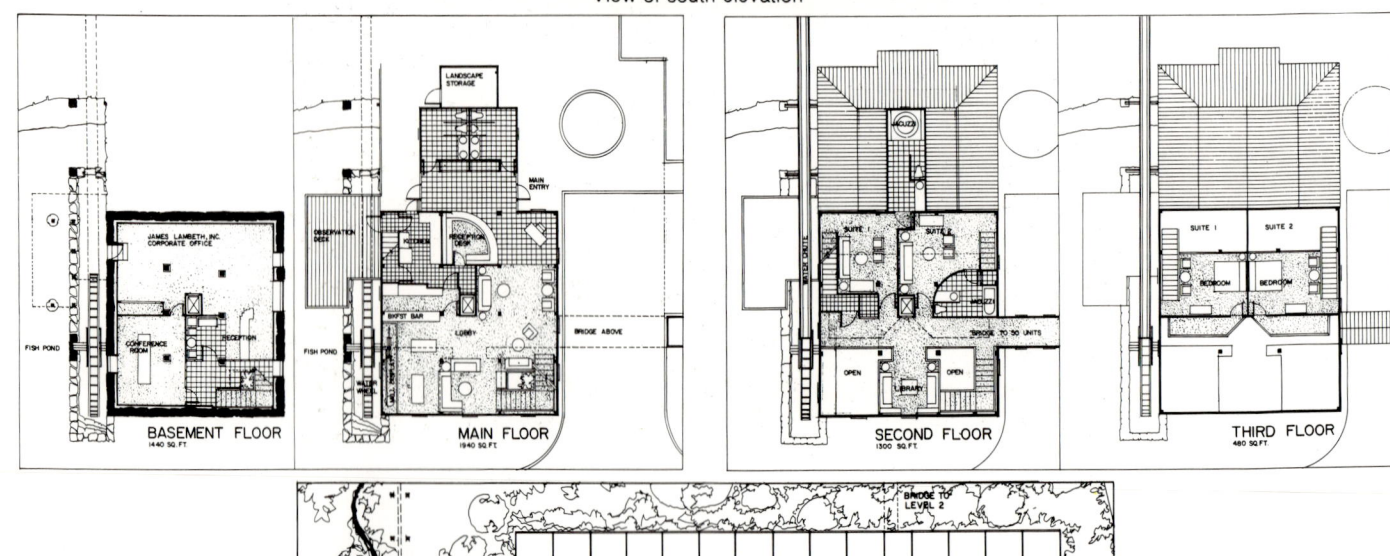

View of entry

South Elevation

Above: Looking down from top balcony   Opposite: Lobby view looking up

Reception with Frank Lloyd Wright window

Mill works and breakfast bar

Stairway with Julie McGinnis quilt

Above: Mill settees of marble and leather

Opposite: Optical illusion of complete curve

Lighting fixture portrait of Courtney Lambeth

East Elevation

Lambeth Residence and Guest House
Fayetteville, Arkansas, 1992, Latitude 36.03N

Recently James Lambeth enlarged his home, adding an art gallery, greenhouse, garages, gatehouse and a guest house.

Adding to the existing structure was problematic because the original house was a balanced, finite design. The solution was to bridge the new and old structures, keeping the addition bi-level and preserving the focus and predominance of the original structure.

The materials chosen were the same as those used in the early home with the addition of glass block. The block appears in a spaced cadence, then forms a two level, half-cylinder containing the greenhouse. There is generous use of marble on both interior and exterior surfaces. The upper level gallery houses Lambeth's collection of Pop Art by artists such as Warhol, Rosenquist, Trova, Stella and Rauschenberg.

Seven garages are broken by a bouldered waterway, at which is featured "Walking Man #2," a stainless steel sculpture by artist Ernest Trova.

The composition is terminated by a two-level guest house. This home turns its back to the street intersection to the northeast with a curving rear wall of black brick. The fortress-like wall is marked by a gridded band of glass block and marble ending in a two-level elevator shaft of alternating brick and glass block.

The auto entry gate is composed of a glass disc etched with a Fourteenth-century sun design set within a triangular metal frame.

The new structure is glassed on the south and cuts into the northern slope, providing protection from the winter north wind.

The central radius point of the guest house composition is a two-story oak tree that extends from the lower entry to the second level ceiling, its branches holding the principal beam of the living room.

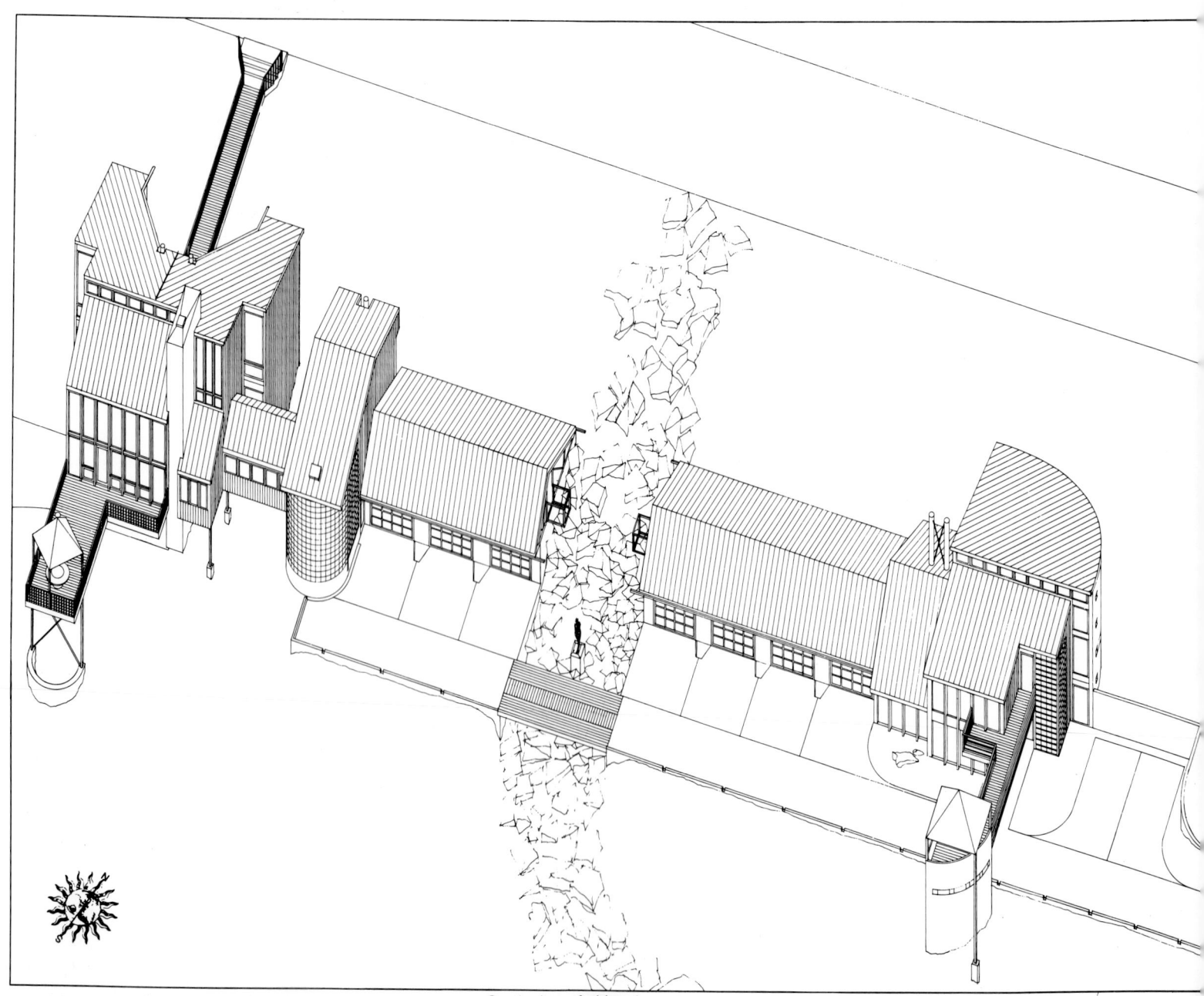

South view of old and new house

View looking west

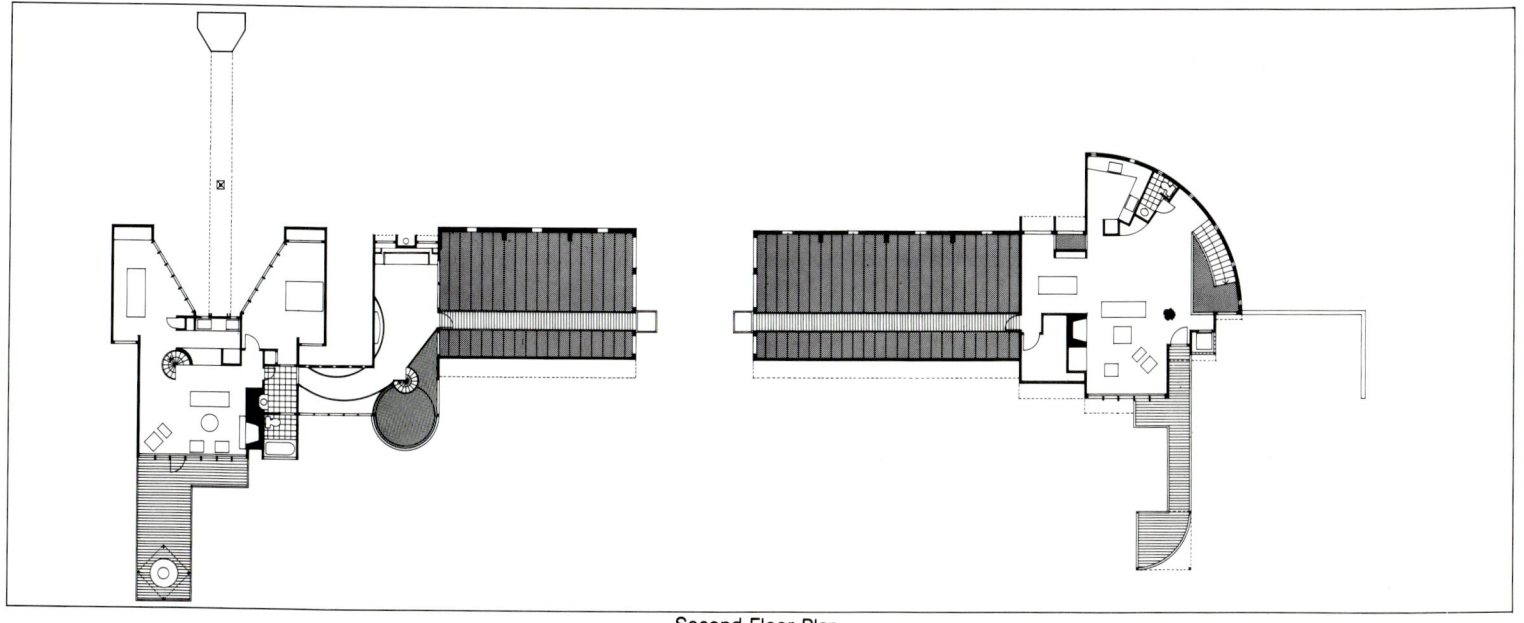
Second Floor Plan

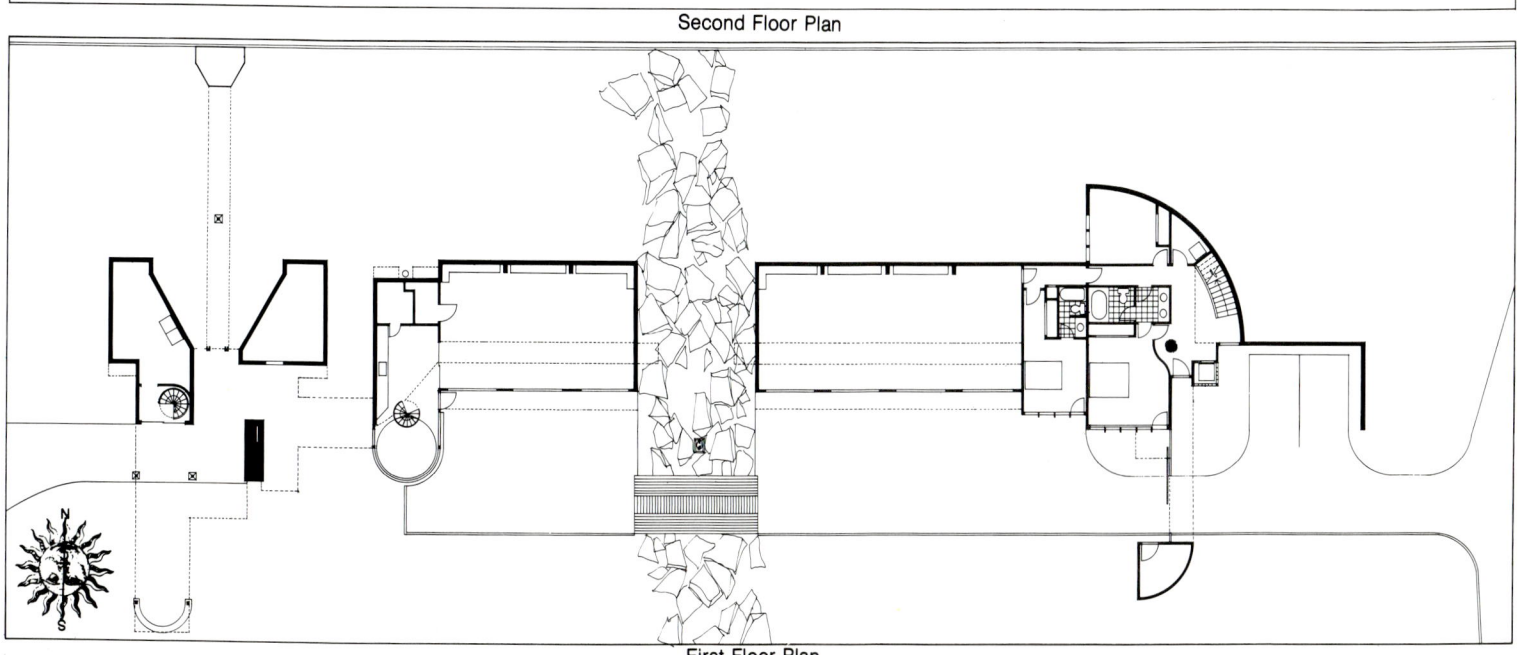
First Floor Plan

Waterway

View of bridge/office

Opposite: View of Gallery looking southeast

View of Ernest Trova "Carman"

Opposite: View of Gallery looking west

Above: Guest house entry lobby with tree trunk Opposite: Living room with tree looking east

Living room looking south

Master bath with Frank Lloyd Wright windows

Above: View of Guest House fireplace

Following Page: Twilight view of east elevation

Entry gate

Selected Bibliography
Books and Articles

C. Ray Smith, "Megastructure Focus,"
PROGRESSIVE ARCHITECTURE, October 1969, p. 177

Norma Conner, "James Lambeth, Residence,"
NORTHWEST ARKANSAS TIMES, January 21, 1971

Barbara Plumb, "Looking Glass Home,"
AMERICAN HOME, March 1971, pp. 61-65

James A. Murphy, "Reflecting Images,"
PROGRESSIVE ARCHITECTURE, May 1971, pp. 112-113

Marta Siemek Espanet, "La villa del ponte,"
INTERNI, Giugno 1971, pp. 12-14, (Italy)

"Lambeth and Belzung Residences,"
TOSHI JUTAKU, cover, September 1971, pp. 120-126, (Japan)

Robin Middleton, "Winter Sun,"
ARCHITECTURAL DESIGN, March 1972, p. 142, (Great Britain)

James A. Murphy, "Warm-up,"
PROGRESSIVE ARCHITECTURE, May 1972, pp. 84-87

Lisa Licitra Ponti, "Micro-clima con la solari,"
DOMUS, cover, Ottobre 1972, n. 515, pp. 5-6, (Italy)

"Yocum Ski Lodge,"
TOSHI JUTAKU, cover, October 1972, pp. 82-84, (Japan)

Jane Brockman, "The Designs of Prof. Lambeth,"
ARKANSAS TRAVELER, November 3, 1972

"Best work of architects under 35,"
ARCHITECTURAL RECORD, December 1972, p. 121

Lisa Licitra Ponti, "Architettura Solare,"
DOMUS, Novembre 1973, pp. 7-8, (Italy)

Alfred Roth, "Misawa Prefabricated Housing International Awards,"
JAPAN ARCHITECT, September 1973, p. 104, n. 201, (Japan)

"Architect gets world acclaim,"
TULSA DAILY WORLD, May 20, 1973

"Solar Living,"
AIA JOURNAL, June 1973, pp. 11-12

William Marlin, "Solar Living,"
ARCHITECTURAL FORUM, December 1973, p. 72

"Sunlight and Architecture,"
ARCHITECTURAL DESIGN, February 1974, (Great Britain)

Lisa Licitra Ponti, "Nel bosoco facade-miroir,"
DOMUS, Luglio 1974, pp. 26-27, n. 536, (Italy)

Marguerite Villecco, "Solar Power,"
ARCHITECTURE PLUS, September-October 1974, p. 92

Louis Joiner, "To harness the Sun,"
SOUTHERN LIVING, December 1974, p. 216

"Mirror Image,"
POOL NEWS, January 1975, p. 68

Marianne Lorenz, "Casa solare nel Missouri,"
DOMUS, Maggio 1975, pp. 18-19, n. 546, (Italy)

"Excellence in Engineering-Steel Solar Lens,"
DESIGN IN STEEL AWARDS PUBLICATION, 1975, p. 13

"Solar Heated Swimming Pool,"
INDUSTRIAL DESIGN, July/August, 1975, p. 92

"Strawberry Fields Apartments,"
ARCHITECTURAL DESIGN, July, 1975 (Great Britain)

"McKamey Residence,"
TOSHI JATAKU, cover, Winter 1975, pp. 74-75, (Japan)

Lisa Licitra Ponti, "Strawberry Fields,"
DOMUS, Marzo 1976, (Italy)

Alison Sky and Michelle Stone, "Lambeth's Solar Village,"
UNBUILT AMERICA, 1976, McGraw Hill Publishing, New York, NY, pp. 10, 158

Louis Joiner, "Heliothermic Mountain Cabin,"
SOUTHERN LIVING, March 1976, p. 92

"Energia Solare,"
INOSSIDABILE 46, Dicembre 1976, p. 8, (Italy)

Jerry Edgerton, "Solar Heating Right Now,"
MONEY MAGAZINE, November 1976, pp. 49-51

Dan MacMasters, "Strawberry Fields Solar Reflector,"
LOS ANGELES TIMES HOME MAGAZINES, March 14, 1976, p. 20

Felicia Butsch, "Solar Energy Cabin,"
PROGRESSIVE FARMER, January 1977, p. 106

Joseph A. Demkin, AIA, "The Delap House, Case Study #7,"
AIA ENERGY NOTEBOOK, 1977-date, AIA Publishing, Washington D.C., pp. CS31

Marguerite Villecco, "Architecture As Energy,"
DESIGN QUARTERLY, Volume 103, 1977, pp. 33-34

Bo Niles/Nina Williams, "Sun Power,"
AMERICAN HOME, January 1977, pp. 34-36

Dave Edmark, "Teacher works with Sun,"
SPRINGDALE NEWS, February 27, 1977

"Solar designs of Professor James Lambeth,"
ART AND ARCHITECTURE, Spring 1977, pp. 37-38, (Iran)

C. Ray Smith, "Illusion and Form,"
SUPERMANNERISM, 1977, Dutton Press, New York, NY, pp. 144-145

Richard G. Stein, FAIA, "Solar Designing, a book review,"
AIA JOURNAL, September 1977, p. 60

"Cabine solaire en montagne/Delap Residence/Village solaire,"
L'ARCHITECTURE d'AUJOURD'HUI, September 1977, pp. 37-42, (France)

David Baier, "Architect-Cover Boy,"
TULSA WORLD, November 14, 1977

Barbara Plumb, "The James Lambeth Residence,"
HOUSES ARCHITECTS LIVE IN, 1977, Viking Press, New York, NY, pp. 156-159

"Dewar's Profile, Scotch Advertisement,"
TIME, NEWSWEEK, HORIZONS, THE NEW YORKER, October thru December, 1977

"Solar Designing, editor's choice/best architectural titles of 1977,"
AIA JOURNAL, November 1977, pp. 46, 64

F.A. Wade, "Solar Homes,"
HORIZONS USA 23, Published by US Information Agency, 1978, p. 12

Donald Watson, AIA, "Aspen Ski Lodge & Strawberry Fields,"
THE SOLAR HOUSE, 1977, Garden Way Publishing, New York, NY, pp. 43, 44

Michael Holtz, "Delap, Richards, Shelton, and Solar Module,"
A SURVEY OF PASSIVE SOLAR BUILDINGS, AIA Research Corp., 1978, pp. 29-31

Ellen Graham, "Dewars Do'ers,"
WALL STREET JOURNAL, August 1, 1978

"An aesthetic approach to solar design,"
PROCESS ARCHITECTURE #6, 1978, pp. 176-181, 73-80, (Japan)

F.A. Wade, "Solar Energy for Homes,"
AMEPNKA, (American Illustrated, Russian Edition), 1978, p. 7, (Russia)

Louis Gropp, "Passive Solar Systems,"
SOLAR HOUSES, 1978, Pantehon Books, New York, NY, pp. 26-27

James Clark, "Architecture's reputation for quality education,"
ARKANSAS ALUMNUS, cover, February 1978, p. 11

"Book Review: Solar Designing,"
DOMUS, Marzo, 1978, p. 56, (Italy)

Editors of Hudson Home Guides, "The Delap Residence,"
A PRACTICAL GUIDE TO SOLAR HOMES, 1978, Bantam/Hudson
Publshing, New York, NY

Lois Blake, "Snowmass Lifestyles,"
SNOWMASS AFFAIRS, March-April 1978, pp. 24-25

Ken Butti, "Solar Architecture,"
ENVIRONMENTAL COMMUNICATIONS, 1979, p. 16

Peter Clegg and Derry Watkins, "Sunspace,"
THE COMPLETE GREENHOUSE BOOK, 1978, Garden Way
Publishing, New York, NY

Anna Fay Friedlander, "Passive takes on many forms,"
SOLAR ENGINEERING MAGAZINE, January 1979, pp. 3, 22-24

"Fellows 1979-80: James Lambeth,"
AMACADEMY, (newsletter/American Academy in Rome) 1978

Vittoria Alliata, "Pannelli Solari Portatili,"
DOMUS, Giugno 1979, p. 49, n. 595, (Italy)

Richard Rush, "Energy Conscious Design,"
PROGRESSIVE ARCHITECTURE, April 1979, p. 145

"Un impianto solare 'passivo'e uno'attivo,"
CASA VOGUE, Ottobre 1979, p. 241, n. 99, (Italy)

"Dr. Benjamin Spock Residence,"
RESEARCH & DESIGN, January 1979, p. 11

"James Lambeth: Passive Solar,"
ARKANSAS GAZETTE, December 12, 1979

Ching-Yu Chang, "The Lambeth House,"
TOSHI JUTAKU, 1980, pp. 124-125, n. 8307, (Japan)

"Energie-Architektur-Wende,"
BAUKULTUR, April 1980, cover, (Germany)

"The Art and Architecture of James Lambeth,"
ANNUAL EXHIBITION PUBLICATION, pp. 27, 28
The American Academy in Rome, 1980, (Italy)

John Hart, "American Academy in Rome Exhibition,"
DAILY AMERICAN, (Rome Edition), Wednesday, May 23, 1979, p. 5,
(Italy)

Ann Wilson, "Passive Solar Power,"
RESIDENTIAL INTERIORS, May/June 1980, pp. 10, 96

Thomas Vonier, "Gorman Towers,"
PROGRESSIVE ARCHITECTURE, May 1980, pp. 48-50

Beverly Russell, "James Lambeth's Solar Interiors,"
INTERIORS, June 1980, p. 9

Jean-Pierre Menard, "Ecole sup'erieur de Blevine, Ark.,"
L'ARCHITECTURE d'AUJOURD'HUI, Juin 1980, pp. 2, 92-93, n. 209,
(France)

"The Passive Solar Interior,"
DESIGNERS WEST, June 1980, pp. 52, 314-318

"Daylighting,"
DESIGNERS WEST, October 1980, pp. 62-67

Dick Grogan, "Solar energy advocate,"
IRISH TIMES, February 2, 1981, (Ireland)

"Solar Reflectivity,"
PROCESS ARCHITECTURE #21, 1981, pp. 56-69, (Japan)

Sarah P. Harkness, "The Solar Section: Starting Point of Passive
Design,"
AIA JOURNAL, January 1981, pp. 68-69

"Energia/Barcelona,"
EL CORREO CATALAN, January 18, 1981, (Spain)

"Solar 4-Architektur + Energie,"
BERLINER KUNSTBLATT, 1981, p. 34, n. 29, (Germany)

"Extraits du 'Conte du Soleil,'"
DOCU BULLETIN, May 1981, cover, pp. 5, 7, n. 5, (Switzerland)

Lynn Walker, "Exhibition of Solar Design,"
THE SPECTRUM, February 13, 1981

William Lake Douglas, "Under Glass,"
LANDSCAPE ARCHITECTURE, January 1982, pp. 92-93

John Spraggins, "Solarmen: A New Breed,"
ARKANSAS TIMES, January 1982, p. 20

Pamela Heyne, "The Solar Mirror,"
TODAY'S ARCHITECTURAL MIRROR, 1982, Van Nostrand Reinhold,
NY, pp. 153-156

"Passive Solar 'Snow Plow,'"
NEW SHELTER, March 1982, p. 92

Christine Winter, "Putting the sun to work,"
CHICAGO TRIBUNE, Monday, April 19, 1982

Charles Jencks, "Strawberry Fields Solar Lens,"
ARCHITECTURE TODAY, 1982, Harry N. Abrams, Inc., New York,
NY, p. 274

"Plowing Snow with Sunlight,"
SCIENCE DIGEST, December 1982, p. 24

Michael/Wedy Wachberger, "Two Projects for Solar Villages,"
ENTWRUF UND PLANUNG, 1983, pp. 122-125, 130-131, (Germany)

"Snow 'Plowed' with Sunlight,"
CURRENT SCIENCE, March 1983, p. 11

Michael Wachberger, "Solar Architecture of James Lambeth,"
E+P, 1983, Staatl .Bef+Beeid Ziviltechniker, Wien, (Austria) p.12

"Solar Designing: Realities and Fantasies,"
RESOURCE, April, 1984

"Sonnenreflektion,"
SOLAR-ARCHITEKTUR, September 1984, p. 11, (Germany)

Marion Long, "Theres no business like snow business,"
FAMILY WEEKLY, (newspaper magazine), February 24, 1985

Mike Trimble, "The Sundance Kid grows up,"
ARKANSAS TIMES, October, 1989, pp. 42-48

Le Roy Donald, "Johnson Mill,"
ARKANSAS GAZETTE, January 23, 1991

Heidi Stambuck, "Johnson Mill, another life,"
THE MORNING NEWS, February 4, 1991

Patricia May, "124-year-old mill in restoration,"
ARKANSAS, INC., February 25, 1991

Kay B. Hall, "Inn at the Mill,"
NORTHWEST ARKANSAS TIMES, May 5, 1991

Heidi Stambuck, "Inn at the Mill now open,"
THE MORNING NEWS, May 23, 1991

Sun Charts

A. June 22
B. May 22 - July 22
C. April 22 - August 22
D. March 22 - Sept. 22
E. Feb. 22 - Oct. 22
F. Jan. 22 - Nov. 22
G. December 22

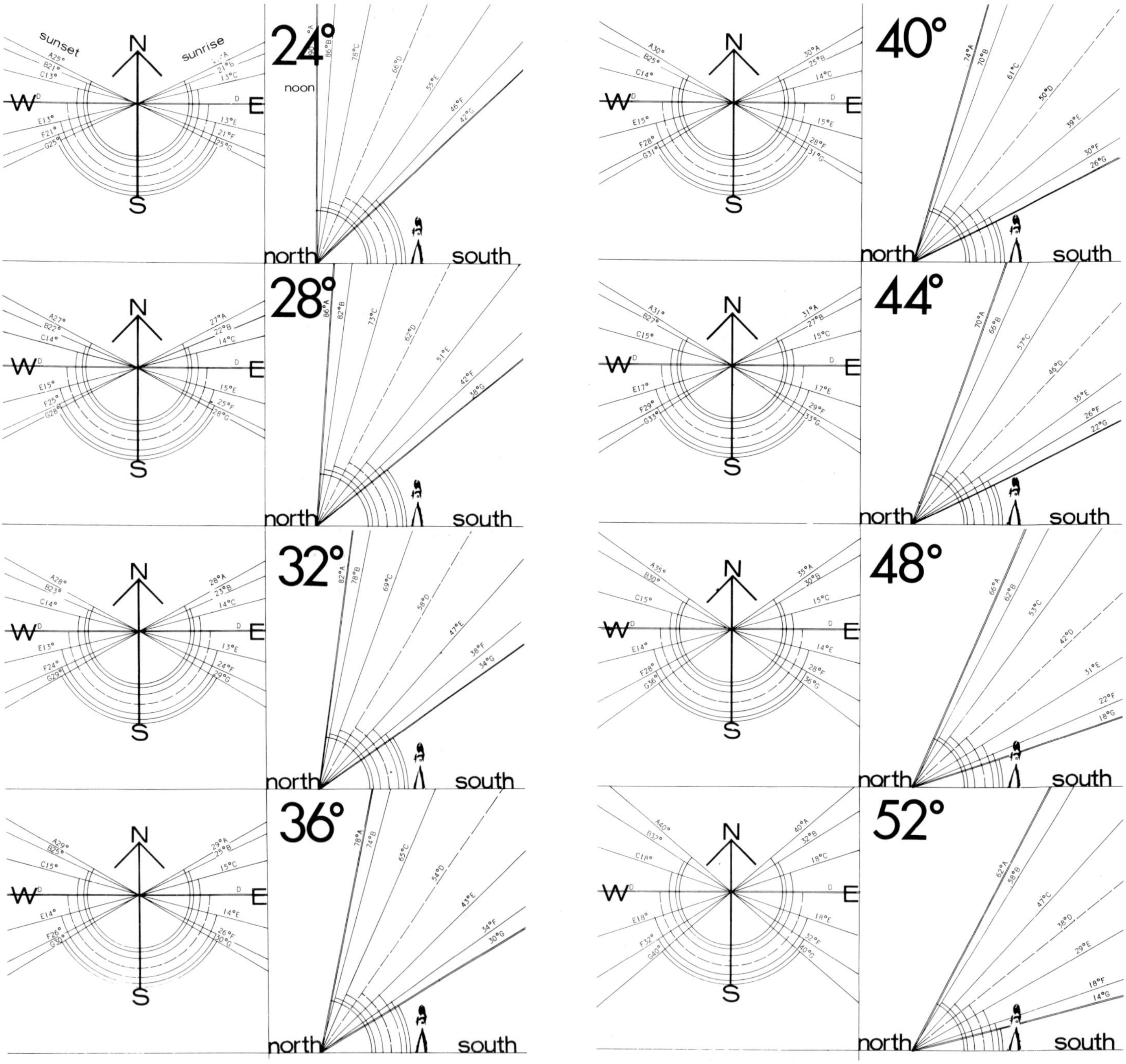

24° Latitude/Calcutta, India/Miami, Florida/Monterrey, Mexico. 28° Latitude/Las Palmas, Canary Islands/Houston, Texas/New Delhi, India. 32° Latitude/Shang-hai, China/Tel Aviv, Israel/Dallas, Texas. 36° Latitude/Tokyo, Japan/Tehran, Iran/Kwang-Ju, Korea/Fayetteville, Arkansas. 40° Latitude/Madrid, Spain/Denver, Colorado/Olympus, Greece/Philadelphia, Pennsylvania. 44° Latitude/Florence, Italy/Auburn, Maine/Alma Ata, Russia. 48° Latitude/Munich, Germany/Budapest, Hungary/Seattle, Washington. 52° Latitude/London, England/Warsaw, Poland/Berlin, Germany.

Acknowledgments

PHOTO CREDITS

All photos are by the Architect except the following; M. Moose, 17, Douglas Kirkland, 49, 64, Larry Logan, 63, Dan/Betty Samples, 137, Richard Leo Johnson, 70, 136, 138, 140, 141, 142, 143, 146, 148, 153, 154, 155, 158, 163, 177, 179, 180, 181, 182, 183, A. Hayes, 208

James Lambeth would like to thank the following for their association on various projects; Hun Bae Im, Pat Harrison, Henry Konover, Mort Karp, Richard Hall, Walter Lehle, Frank McMillin, Larry Phillips, Michael Saar, Robert Schraplau, Dallas Taylor, Richard Dagenhart, Doug Bryant, Roger Critz, Peter Connelly, James Parker, Kent Davis, John Delap, John Booth, Gregory Davis, Paul Gregory, David Lewis, Benson Lowe, Mercedes Stadthagen, Jon Steele, Shahla Taratabai and Gary Lambeth.

James Lambeth would like to thank the writers who have so generously covered his ideas over the past twenty years. Also the incredibly brave clients who allowed the fantasies to become realities. And finally to the craftsmen who applied their skills and labor to realize these designs, especially Ray Smith and Ed Hines for their intelligence and patience.

ABOUT THE EDITORS

Hun Bae Im is an architectural engineer, a graduate of Yon Sei University of Seoul, Korea and the University of Arkansas. He has been an associate with James Lambeth on many projects and is an authority on Lambeth's work. He lives with his wife in Fayetteville, Arkansas.

Born in Fayetteville, Arkansas, Courtney Lambeth studied the history of art and architecture at Vassar College and continued her graduate studies at Sotheby's in London. She lives and works in Santa Fe, New Mexico.

James Lambeth, AIA, FAAR, was born in Kansas City, Missouri in 1942. He attended Washington University in St. Louis and Rice University in Houston. In 1978 he won the Prix de Rome in Architecture, his fellowship funded by the National Endowment for the Arts. He was a professor of Architecture at the University of Arkansas for 20 years.

His architecture has been published internationally. He has been a design consultant to the Vatican, NASA, Time-Life, Union Carbide, National Geographic, and Disney.

He lives with his wife, Joyce, in Fayetteville, Arkansas, and in Miami, Florida.